How Do
I KNOW IF
I Know?

How Do
I KNOW IF
I Know?

JOHN BYTHEWAY

DESERET
BOOK

Salt Lake City, Utah

*To Ashley, Andrew, Natalie,
Matthew, Timothy, and Bethany*

Library of Congress Cataloging-in-Publication Data

Bytheway, John, author.
    How do I know if I know? / John Bytheway.
        pages cm
    Includes bibliographical references.
    ISBN 978-1-60907-921-5 (paperbound)
1. Witness bearing (Christianity)—The Church of Jesus Christ of Latter-day Saints. 2. Spiritual life—The Church of Jesus Christ of Latter-day Saints. 3. The Church of Jesus Christ of Latter-day Saints—Doctrines. 4. Mormon Church—Doctrines. I. Title.
    BX8643.T45B98   2014
    248.4'89332—dc23   2014016978

Printed in the United States of America
Publishers Printing, Salt Lake City, UT

10   9   8   7   6   5   4   3

Contents

What Do You Know?

Many years ago, a young man (he was only twenty-three years old) was called to be the new stake president in Tooele, Utah. In those days, stake conferences had two sessions, and at lunch between the sessions, Joseph F. Smith, one of the General Authorities attending, said to the new stake president, "You said you believe the gospel with all your heart, and propose to live it, but you did not bear your testimony that you know it is true. Don't you know absolutely that this gospel is true?"

"I do not," answered the young man.

"President Taylor," said Elder Smith to the President of the Church, John Taylor, who was also in attendance, "I am in favor of undoing this afternoon what we did this morning. I do not think any man should preside over a stake who has not a perfect and abiding knowledge of the divinity of this work."

President Taylor just laughed and said, "Joseph, Joseph, Joseph, he knows it just as well as you do. The only thing that he does not know is that he does know it."

That story brings up a very interesting question: Is it possible to know that the Church is true, but not *know* that you know? Is a testimony that hard to detect? This story is even more interesting when you learn the identity of the new stake president. His name was Heber J. Grant. Yes, the same Heber J. Grant who later became the President of the Church.[1]

Interestingly, the next time Heber J. Grant faced members of his stake, he spoke powerfully for forty-five minutes. This time, he knew. And he *knew* that he knew. What did President Grant do in between "believing" the Church was true and "knowing"? And how can we do the same thing?

Today, youth and young adults are facing huge decisions, and they're facing them a little sooner than their older brothers and sisters did. Many teenagers facing the mission decision may be wondering, "Is my testimony strong enough? Do I really know the Church is true? How do I know if I know?" Because of the lowering of the age at which young people become eligible to serve missions, there is a greater urgency than ever before to answer this kind of question. I once heard Sister Sheri Dew tell a group of young people, "We want you to figure out what we've figured out, and we want you to figure it out *quicker* than we figured it out."

Spiritual Gut Check: Why We Must *Know* That We Know

What are the biggest problems facing the members of the Church today? Immorality? Pornography? Drugs? Worldliness? Idleness? No. Those are secondary problems. Those temptations lose much of their power if we solve the *real* problem. The real problem is weak testimonies. Elder Vaughn J. Featherstone observed:

> Number one on our agenda, above all else, is faith in Christ. I don't know anything that will take the place of it. Whenever we find problems in the Church, we usually find them under one of

two umbrellas or canopies, either transgression or lack of faith in Christ.[2]

What the members of the Church need, more than anything else, are strong testimonies of Jesus Christ and the gospel He restored. They need to know. And they need to know that they know. This is the best protection against the tsunami of temptations and the waves of immorality that crash against us. Perhaps this is just another reason why the first principle of the gospel is faith in the Lord Jesus Christ!

What Is a Testimony, Anyway?

If we want to gain, discover, or rekindle a testimony, we'd better know exactly what it is. *True to the Faith* describes a testimony as "a spiritual witness given by the Holy Ghost."[3] Yet some of us are unsure how to recognize the Holy Ghost when it is present, or we believe that the Spirit must come in a certain way. Some people share amazing spiritual experiences about how, in one moment, they receive a powerful witness. They hear a voice, or feel an overwhelming sense of peace and assurance, or experience a burning in their hearts. Others speak of their testimonies growing slowly, or "line upon line," as time goes by, but they cannot point to a specific day or event when they suddenly knew what they didn't know before. Still others say, "Oh, I can't really say when I gained my testimony; I guess I've just always known." Then, perhaps, there's another category—President Grant's category—those who know, but who don't know that they know! This book was written mostly for them, and for anyone else who wonders if his or her testimony is strong enough to survive and thrive in this world.

The first syllable of the word *testimony* is "test," and yes, there is a test in acquiring the knowledge you seek. But whatever you do, please don't be discouraged on this quest! The Lord wants to send His Spirit to you—He wants you to know! But He also wants you to act in faith and to move forward even when you don't know. So the important thing is that you keep trying. It's obvious that you are trying, because you're reading this book!

A Testimony Is Like . . .

My friend Brad Wilcox suggests that we shouldn't speak of testimonies using "light switch" terminology such as it's "on" or it's "off"; " I have a testimony" or "I don't have a testimony"; "I had it, but I lost it." A testimony is not an all-or-nothing proposition. There are different levels of testimony, and our testimonies can grow or dwindle based on our experiences, our circumstances, and our choices.

A testimony is a mixture of things we know, things we feel, things we believe, things we hope for, and maybe even things we doubt! Perhaps this is why the man seeking a blessing for his son told the Savior, "Lord, I believe; help thou mine unbelief" (Mark 9:24). This man, like many of us, believed some things for sure, but he also had some doubts, or some "unbelief." Most important, he wanted help, and he went to the Savior—he wanted to believe more! If we have some doubts, or some "unbelief," we should go to the Savior too.

A Flash or a Sunrise

If your testimony doesn't come in a flash, don't be concerned. Yes, some have received powerful spiritual experiences in one bright moment. Paul saw Jesus on the road to Damascus, Enos prayed all day and was visited of the Lord, and King Lamoni said a prayer and was suddenly overcome. These experiences were so remarkable they've been preserved forever in the scriptures! Some young people conclude, "Wow, nothing like that has ever happened to me. I guess I don't have a testimony." President Ezra Taft Benson corrected that type of thinking when he warned:

> We must be cautious as we discuss these remarkable examples. Though they are real and powerful, they are the exception more than the rule. For every Paul, for every Enos, and for every King Lamoni, there are hundreds and thousands of people who find the process of repentance much more subtle, much more imperceptible. Day by day they move closer to the Lord, little realizing they are building a godlike life. They live quiet lives of goodness, service, and commitment. They are like the Lamanites, who the Lord said "were baptized with fire and with the Holy Ghost, *and they knew it not.*" (3 Ne. 9:20; italics added.)[4]

You would think that if you were "baptized with fire," you would know about it! But that phrase teaches us something about the experience. Yes, it's a "mighty change of heart," but that doesn't mean it's an *instant* change of heart. It took time! For most of us, "hundreds and thousands" of us, a testimony comes more like a sunrise: slowly, subtly, but surely.

Some young people come home from their missions saying things like, "I'm not sure if I grew enough spiritually." Their parents are shocked to hear them say that because they've noticed amazing growth! The version of the son or daughter they dropped off at the MTC is much different from the one who just walked off the plane. But the returned missionary might not have noticed the growth because it happened so slowly, over a couple of years. It was mighty, but not instant.

With a sunrise, it would be hard to pinpoint the exact moment when things go from dark to light because it happens so gradually. It takes a few hours, much longer than a flash. (That reminds me of a joke: "I wondered all night where the sun went—then it dawned on me!") It's true, the morning doesn't break in an instant, but you can see it gradually coming for hours. Then, it dawns on you.

Elder David A. Bednar compared "light switch" experiences to "sunrise" experiences when he taught:

A light turned on in a dark room is like receiving a message from God quickly, completely, and all at once. Many of us have experienced this pattern of revelation as we have been given answers to sincere prayers or been provided with needed direction or protection, according to God's will and timing. Descriptions of such immediate and intense manifestations are found in the scriptures, recounted in Church history, and evidenced in our own lives. Indeed, these mighty miracles do occur. *However, this pattern of revelation tends to be more rare than common.* The gradual increase of light radiating from the rising sun is like receiving a message from God "line upon line, precept upon precept" (2 Nephi 28:30). Most frequently, revelation comes in small increments over time and is granted according to our desire, worthiness, and preparation. . . . *This pattern of revelation tends to be more common than rare.*[5]

So, if you've never had a "flash of light" type of experience, you're in good company. Most of us haven't. And that's okay—again, it's part of the "test" in testimony. Remember, "ye receive no witness until after the trial of your faith" (Ether 12:6).

Give Me a Second for My Eyes to Adjust

Oddly enough, some who have been raised in the Church or who have been around the Spirit all their lives may be wondering if they even have a testimony at all because they are expecting something different, or something more—a level of light they haven't experienced. Perhaps they think it has to come in one amazing moment, like a bolt of lightning, or with a vision. They may come to realize, like President Grant, that they've known all along.

Elder Glenn L. Pace commented on those who have been born and raised in the light of day and don't realize how bright it is:

> When seeking a testimony, those of you born into the Church may be looking for some spectacular spiritual feeling different than anything you have ever felt before. You may have heard converts testify of their conversion and wonder if you're missing something. One reason it seems so spectacular to them is that it is new. You have

had the same feelings your whole life during family home evenings, youth testimony meetings, seminary classes, scripture reading, and on many other occasions.[6]

For a convert, discovering the truths of the gospel might be like going from dim light to bright light, and the contrast would be unmistakable. For example, while I was working on this book, I had a meeting in downtown Salt Lake City, and I parked underneath the new City Creek mall. When I was leaving, maneuvering around looking for the exit, I was thinking what a good job they did designing the parking plaza. It was bright and roomy, and I didn't feel like I was in a cave. When I found my way to the exit ramp and drove out of the underground plaza into the daylight, I was shocked—the sun was so bright it actually hurt my eyes! As I was reaching for my sunglasses, I noticed that other drivers emerging from the dark were having the same experience. It was brighter outside, much brighter than I expected it to be. Just a few moments before, when I was underground, it hadn't seemed dark, but now I knew there was a much brighter light outside. The people already outside walking down the sidewalk weren't in pain, but I was. They were used to the light, but for those first few moments, I wasn't. Perhaps you've been surrounded by the Spirit all your life, and you've come to think of it as normal. Someone else might be plopped into your situation and exclaim, "Whoa, what is this feeling?" Many of us have been out walking in the sunshine, not realizing we've enjoyed the light all along. Elder Joseph B. Wirthlin taught:

> A testimony of the truth of the gospel does not come the same way to all people. Some receive it in a unique, life-changing experience. Others gain a testimony slowly, almost imperceptibly until, one day, they simply know.[7]

Still, we need to know, and we need to know that we know. Brother Wilcox is right, a testimony is not like a light switch with only two settings, on or off. So what is a testimony like? For the rest of this book, I'm going to suggest that a testimony is more like a light with a dimmer switch that makes possible an almost infinite number of settings between total light and total darkness. Just as there are levels of light, there are levels of testimony as well. The following chart starts with the darkness of unbelief and grows brighter and brighter until it reaches the top.

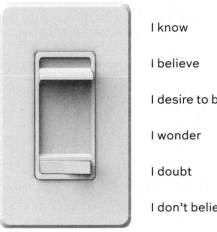

I know

I believe

I desire to believe

I wonder

I doubt

I don't believe

With the dimmer switch, we can see how someone could have some light, some belief, yet still say, "I desire more light," or "help thou mine unbelief." You may encounter people on your mission who simply do not believe, but if they are willing to suspend disbelief just for a moment, something happens. As you teach and testify, and as the Spirit begins to "enlighten" their minds, they may move from doubt to wondering, and from wondering to a "desire to believe" (Alma

32:27). Over time, their desire may grow into a belief, and then even a knowledge that what they have learned about the gospel is good and true. As you let your light shine in their lives, it may turn their darkness into day.

The Lord spoke of a "growing light" in this interesting verse of scripture that perfectly fits our dimmer-switch analogy:

> That which is of God is light; and he that receiveth light, and continueth in God, receiveth more light; and that light groweth brighter and brighter until the perfect day. (D&C 50:24)

That is our goal: to take the light we have, to "continue in God" and gain more, to grow brighter and brighter until the perfect day, or until we can say, "I really do know."

A Christmas Tree

One young woman at a testimony meeting impressed me when she said, "I don't have a testimony of everything, but I have a testimony of enough." Her comment made me think of another way to describe a testimony. So far, we've talked about a testimony as one overall belief. But our "overall testimony" may consist of many "individual testimonies" of certain principles. We may have a strong testimony of the Word of Wisdom, for example, but we're still working on a testimony of the law of tithing. We may believe the Book of Mormon is true, but we're still working on gaining a testimony of the priesthood being restored. There may be doctrines that we don't understand yet. But we have a testimony of the basics—God is real; He lives and loves us. Jesus Christ is His Son and our Savior. The gospel has been restored.

Let's say a testimony of an individual truth is like a tiny bulb on a Christmas tree. Add another tiny truth, and there's more light. Add another, still more, and a tree of a hundred tiny 1-watt lights brightens the whole room! Don't be discouraged if some lights haven't lit up yet, because in this particular string of lights, just because one is out it doesn't mean they're all out, or that the others can't shine! Even for adults there are always new things to learn and new things to ask the Lord about. I don't think there is anyone who will know everything there is to know about the gospel in this life. But each of us can have a bright, burning testimony of what we do know, and we can have it now!

So whether we're thinking of a dimmer switch connected to a 100-watt bulb or a Christmas tree with a hundred 1-watt bulbs, our desire is the same—to grow brighter, or to gain further light and knowledge. And to do that, we come to Christ. In this context, it's interesting to remember that Jesus said, "I am the light of the world" (John 8:12). But He also said, "*Ye* are the light of the world" (Matthew 5:14; emphasis added). He is willing to share His name and His light with us so that we will share it with others and "enlighten" the world.

You Shall "F.E.E.L." It Is Right

Not everyone will be enlightened in the same way, but since the Lord loves all of us, we are safe in believing the Lord will communicate to each person in the best way for that individual, according to His wisdom.

Some have powerful *feelings* while pondering the gospel. They may also have *experiences* that teach and verify the truth. Some find great strength from *evidences* of God's involvement in their lives or *evidences* of the truthfulness of the scriptures, and others feel the gospel makes sense and find power in the order or the *logic* of it all. All of these areas feed our testimonies.

So, we might say our dimmer switch draws energy from four different sources, or wires. These sources of power spell the word *FEEL*, and they include:

Feelings	"you shall *feel* that it is right" (D&C 9:8; emphasis added)
Experiences	"If any man will *do* his will, he shall know . . ." (John 7:17; emphasis added)
Evidences	"Ye shall know them by their *fruits*." (Matthew 7:16; emphasis added)
Logic	"I will tell you in your *mind* . . ." (D&C 8:2; emphasis added)

As we talk about each of these sources of testimony, my hope is that you will identify your own feelings, experiences, evidences, and logical conclusions, and that you will feel enlightened, and that your testimony will grow brighter—not only because you've learned new things but because you've been reminded of things you've always known.

Have you ever sung the hymn that starts with the words, "When upon life's billows"? (Whatever "billow" means—as a kid, I preferred "When upon life's pillows.") The song contains some wonderful advice to produce feelings of gratitude—namely, to "count your blessings" and to "name them one by one." The result? It will "*surprise* you what the Lord has done."[8]

As we look at the many different elements of testimony—the feelings, the experiences, the evidences, and the logic—as we talk about them, count them, and "name them one by one," it might just *surprise* you what the Lord has done. And I hope that by the time you reach the last page, you will be able to say, "Wow. I really do know . . . and I know that I know!"

More LIGHT on the subject . . .

Elder David A. Bednar: http://www .mormonchannel.org/video/mormon -messages?v=1737858986001

Notes

1. Heber J. Grant, *Gospel Standards* (Improvement Era, 1941), 192.

2. Vaughn J. Featherstone, "The Torchbearer," *Brigham Young University 1982–83 Fireside and Devotional Speeches* (University Publications, 1983), 145.

3. *True to the Faith* (The Church of Jesus Christ of Latter-day Saints, 2004), 178.

4. Ezra Taft Benson, "A Mighty Change of Heart," *Ensign*, October 1989, 5.

5. David A. Bednar, "The Spirit of Revelation," *Ensign*, May 2011, 88; emphasis added.

6. Glenn L. Pace, "Do You Know?" *Ensign*, May 2007, 78.

7. Joseph B. Wirthlin, "Pure Testimony," *Ensign*, November 2000, 23.

8. "Count Your Blessings," *Hymns* (The Church of Jesus Christ of Latter-day Saints, 1985), no. 241; emphasis added.

Wire One: Feelings

Most often when we talk about testimonies, we refer to feelings. We talk about "feeling the Spirit," or "feeling good" about a decision, or "feeling impressed" to do something. And yet, when we try to describe how we felt, or exactly what something felt like, we discover it's very hard to explain. President Boyd K. Packer taught:

> We do not have the words (even the scriptures do not have words) which perfectly describe the Spirit. The scriptures generally use the word *voice*, which does not exactly fit. These delicate, refined spiritual communications are not seen with our eyes nor heard with our ears. And even though it is described as a voice, it is a voice that one feels more than one hears.[1]

"Feeling" the Spirit takes practice, patience, and persistence. Many of us have felt it, but we haven't recognized it. In other words, we know, but we don't know that we know. Learning to feel the Spirit is a lifelong process. So how does the Spirit feel?

Feeling the Burning in the Bosom

Perhaps the feeling described most often when discussing a testimony is a "burning in the bosom." This expression is used in the Doctrine and Covenants regarding the translation process for the Book of Mormon (see D&C 9:8). It's also used in the New Testament, describing the time when the resurrected Jesus walked along the road to Emmaus with two disciples who didn't recognize Him. After Jesus departed, they said to one another, "Did not our heart burn within us, while he talked with us by the way, and while he opened to us the scriptures?" (Luke 24:32).

Many of us hope for, long for, and pray for this type of "burning," powerful witness, and some of us get discouraged when it doesn't come. We might even feel ashamed or worry that we are less spiritual than others because we've never had our heart burn within us. Our mistake is when we assume that a witness of the Spirit *must* be the burning in the bosom. If you have never felt the burning feeling described by these verses, it doesn't mean that you've never had a witness, that you're not worthy, or that you don't have a testimony. Don't be discouraged; you're in good company. Elder Dallin H. Oaks taught:

> I have met persons who told me they have never had a witness from the Holy Ghost because they have never felt their bosom "burn within" them. What does a "burning in the bosom" mean? Does it need to be a feeling of caloric heat, like the burning produced by combustion? If that is the meaning, I have never had a burning in the bosom. Surely, the word "burning" in this scripture signifies a feeling of comfort and serenity. That is the witness many receive. That is the way revelation works. Truly, the still, small voice is just that, "still" and "small."[2]

Elder Jay E. Jensen shared this comment from another member of the Quorum of the Twelve:

> As I have traveled throughout the Church, I've found relatively few people who have

experienced a burning of the bosom. In fact, I've had many people tell me that they've become frustrated because they have never experienced that feeling even though they have prayed or fasted for long periods of time.[3]

I know people who say they have felt this burning feeling, but I also know many who have never felt it. And that's okay! Have you ever heard someone say, "That's a heartwarming story"? Do they literally mean their heart felt warm, or is it just an expression? Perhaps the "burning in the bosom" can range anywhere from a heartwarming feeling to a feeling of physical heat.

One of the most important principles to learn in your quest for spiritual knowledge is that the Lord communicates differently to different people. Again, a witness of the Spirit is not limited to only the "burning" feeling. Let's talk about some of the other feelings that may come when we feel the Spirit.

Feelings of Joy

Lehi told his son Jacob, "Men are, that they might have joy" (2 Nephi 2:25). When the Spirit of the Lord is present, people are happier. You can see it in their faces, in the way they carry themselves, and in their lives. If it's really true that "wickedness never was happiness" (Alma 41:10), then doesn't it make sense that God, who is righteous, pure, and holy, would be happy? And wouldn't we feel happy when we feel His Spirit? Heber C. Kimball taught:

> I am perfectly satisfied that my Father and my God is a cheerful, pleasant, lively, good-natured Being. Why? Because I am cheerful, pleasant, lively, and good-natured when I have His Spirit. That is one reason why I know; and another is—the Lord said, through Joseph Smith, "I delight in a glad heart and a cheerful countenance." That arises from the perfection of His attributes; He is a jovial, lively person, and a beautiful man.[4]

To me, one of the happiest places on the planet is not a Southern California amusement park (although I like that, too), but the temple. I always feel calm, serene, peaceful, and happy within the walls of the temple. I've also noticed how many smiling faces I see there. The feeling is strong, and it's quite a contrast with being almost anywhere else on earth. It is a testimony to me. Sometimes I wish I could just sit there all day.

Many people, when they leave the temple doors and make their way to the parking lot, give a heavy sigh and say, "back to the real world." Elder John H. Groberg heard someone use that expression, and responded:

> I understand your feelings, but actually, it is the other way around. You are not leaving the temple and going back into the *real world*, you are leaving the *real world* (the temple) and going back in the *unreal* (temporary) world. Only that which lasts forever is *real*. That which is done in the temple lasts forever; therefore, the *temple* is the *real world*. Most of what we experience "out there" such as sickness, wealth, poverty, fame, etc., lasts for only a short period of time, so it is not the *real world*.[5]

The feeling within the temple is a testimony of the temple. Perhaps you've had the opportunity to visit the temple and participate in baptisms for the dead. If so, I suspect you already know it feels different from any other place in the world. Adjectives that come to mind are: *still, quiet, calm, serene, comfortable, peaceful.*

Is "Happy Valley" a Place or a People?

A recent website ranked Brigham Young University as the "7th happiest" college in the nation.[6] Why would that be? The students felt they were part of "something bigger," and that contributed to their happiness. As a graduate of Brigham Young University, I can attest that it is another one of my favorite places on earth. For me, it just feels good being on campus. But maybe you could chalk that up to so-called "school spirit." Is it the campus or the buildings that cause these happy feelings? Or is there something going on in the hearts of the people?

Less than an hour north of BYU is another school I attended called the University of Utah. Eric Weddle is a Latter-day Saint who currently plays football for the San Diego Chargers, but at one time, he was a freshman cornerback for the University of Utah. As his freshman year commenced, he began to notice something about certain of his teammates, who seemed to be unusually happy, even during the strenuous football workouts.

It was during one of these torturous sessions that Eric noticed Morgan Scalley with a smile on his face, as if he were actually having a good time. Scalley's cheerful disposition boggled Eric's mind. "He was jumping around, laughing and yelling like it was fun. Why was he so happy?" Eric said. "I learned there was something more to him, something special."[7]

What was that "something more," that "something special"? Eventually, Eric's questions led to an appointment with the missionaries. Eric's Latter-day Saint friends were afraid the lesson didn't go very well, but to Eric, it was awesome. "I was as happy as can be. It was the calm feeling I felt. I felt like what they were saying was true."[8] Eric was eventually baptized by another teammate, Justin Hansen.

Remember, it all started with Eric noticing how happy someone was, seeing that his friend had "something more." The students interviewed at BYU felt they were part of "something bigger." Eric Weddle recognized "something more," "something special." So, whether it's "something special," "something bigger," or "something more," it is *something!* And it is recognized by others. The "something" described here is evidence of the Spirit of the Lord, a witness of the Holy Ghost, and a testimony of truth.

Does the Spirit Make You Cry?

One young woman who attended Especially for Youth wrote in her evaluation, "I felt the spirit. Not a crying spirit, but a cheerful, excited to learn spirit." That is a witness! Some people feel strong emotion when feeling the Spirit, but it's not always the case. Some people may labor under the delusion, "Whoever cries the most is the most spiritual." Not true! If you watch closely in general conference you will notice—even among the leaders of the Church—some who get a bit emotional and some who don't. We're all different! President Howard W. Hunter counseled seminary teachers:

> I get concerned when it appears that strong emotion or free-flowing tears are equated with the presence of the Spirit. Certainly the Spirit of the Lord can bring strong emotional feelings, including tears, but that outward manifestation

ought not to be confused with the presence of the Spirit itself. I have watched a great many of my brethren over the years, and we have shared some rare and unspeakable spiritual experiences together. Those experiences have all been different, each special in its own way, and such sacred moments may or may not be accompanied by tears. Very often they are, but sometimes they are accompanied by total silence. Other times they are accompanied by joy.[9]

The Spirit and strong emotion are not the same thing. Sometimes they accompany one another, and other times they do not. If you happen to cry as you share your testimony, that's okay, and if you don't, that's okay too! Your emotions are not a measure of your testimony.

Feeling Enlightened

The Doctrine and Covenants mentions the "burning in the bosom" feeling once, but it mentions another feeling much more frequently—the feeling of being *enlightened*. Why would that be? Perhaps the feeling of being enlightened is more common than the burning feeling. Here are a few samples:

Doctrine and Covenants 6:15: Behold, thou knowest that thou hast inquired of me and I did *enlighten* thy mind; and now I tell thee these things that thou mayest know that thou hast been *enlightened* by the Spirit of truth.

Doctrine and Covenants 11:13: Verily, verily, I say unto you, I will impart unto you of my Spirit, which shall *enlighten* your mind, which shall fill your soul with joy.

Doctrine and Covenants 76:10: For by my Spirit will I *enlighten* them, and by my power will I make known unto them the secrets of my will—yea, even those things which eye has not seen, nor ear heard, nor yet entered into the heart of man.

Doctrine and Covenants 84:46: And the Spirit giveth light to every man that cometh into the world; and the Spirit *enlighteneth* every man through the world, that hearkeneth to the voice of the Spirit.

When you're enlightened, you see things you didn't see before. You've probably noticed that the word *light* is the center of the word *enlightened*. Have you also noticed that when a cartoon character gets an idea, the artist draws a lightbulb over the person's head? We even refer to smart people as being "bright" or having a "bright idea." Why is that? Because suddenly we see. (Fun fact: Did you know the flag for Yale University contains Hebrew symbols for "light and truth"? It does. In Latin, the translation is *Lux et Veritas*, but do you know the literal translation of the Hebrew symbols? *Urim and Thummim.* Interesting, huh?)

My favorite word for this "enlightening" witness of the Spirit is *clarity*. In other words, something that was foggy, fuzzy, or confusing becomes clear, sharp, and obvious. I remember a youth conference in Oklahoma where the Spirit was present. A young woman passed me a note, telling me that she suddenly realized she needed to break up with her boyfriend. It was an interesting comment because it was totally out of context. At that point, no one at the youth conference had talked about dating or standards or the law of chastity. But it didn't matter, because the Spirit was present, and it speaks to us individually, and it made certain things clear in her mind. Jacob wrote, "The Spirit speaketh the truth and lieth not. Wherefore, it speaketh of things as they really are, and of things as they really will be" (Jacob 4:13). The witness of the Spirit enlightened that young woman and helped her see things as they really were. It didn't make her heart burn or cause her to cry, but it was nevertheless a spiritual witness. You can probably remember seminary lessons, conference talks, or even moments of personal study when you felt "enlightened." If so, you've received a witness of the Spirit.

The Feeling of Peace

Where can we turn for peace? To the Spirit of the Lord. Jesus told His disciples, just before the events of His trial and Crucifixion, "Peace I leave with you, my peace I give unto you: not as the world giveth, give I unto you. Let not your heart be troubled, neither let it be afraid" (John 14:27).

Jesus was teaching us that there is a kind of peace that the world cannot give. We often call the Spirit the "Comforter" (which is also what we call a warm blanket). Sometimes, we just feel calm and comfortable when the Spirit is present. Oliver Cowdery was seeking a witness of the truth from the Lord, and the Lord sent him another revelation to tell him that he'd already received a revelation:

> If you desire a further witness, cast your mind upon the night that you cried unto me in your heart, that you might know concerning the truth of these things. Did I not speak peace to your mind concerning the matter? What greater witness can you have than from God? (D&C 6:22–23)

These are very important verses of scripture, especially for those of us who are wondering if we've ever felt the Spirit! They let us know that a feeling of calm and peace, a common experience for most of us, is itself a witness. Oliver had received that feeling and evidently didn't consider it a witness. So the Lord spoke again and told him that it was!

While I was serving as bishop, a wonderful senior brother joined the Church. Very often when I arrived at the building, long before our regular meetings were scheduled to start, this man was already sitting in the foyer. He wasn't reading a book or a lesson manual or waiting for an interview; he was just sitting there with a pleasant look on his face. One week, when I asked him why he always came so early, he said he felt peace in the meetinghouse, and he came early each week to sit quietly and enjoy the wonderful feeling.

More than once, I've participated in a youth conference in which a wonderful spirit filled the chapel during a fireside. And more than once, after the closing prayer, I've seen young people stay in their seats and not want to budge an inch. Even with a dance starting up in the cultural hall! They just wanted to stay and soak in the Spirit. I remember one youth conference where some teenagers spent the entire dance time sitting in the chapel. I sat with them, and we talked about wonderful things for over two hours. I hope they knew that they were receiving a witness.

A young woman named Bethany related how she didn't realize how much the Church meant to her until her beliefs were challenged:

> A popular guy I liked from school asked me out on a date. I was thrilled and was flattered to

be singled out. I worked really hard to do the right thing by convincing him to bring another couple along. I was the only member of the Church in the group. We decided to see a movie, so I had to talk everyone into seeing one that was appropriate (so much work for one date!). After the movie, we were all driving home and started talking about church. They asked me about the church I belong to. I was really excited to share something about my faith, but before I could say anything my date burst out that he knew all about Mormons. His sister had done a research paper on our religion and attended church once as part of her research. He then started making fun of the things we believed in. Everyone was laughing and saying hurtful things. I couldn't bear to hear those things said even in misunderstanding. I quickly asked them to stop and the only words I could choke out were that "my church means so much to me." *I didn't know until that moment how strongly I felt about being a member of the Church until I had to stand up for it.* After that I started reading the scriptures more seriously and praying more often. I am so glad I had the "jump start" experience to get my testimony going.[10]

Just as you don't know how strong a cable is until it is tested, some young people haven't known how strong their testimony is, or what it means to them, until it is put to the test.

Feeling Rotten

It can also be a testimony of truth when you *don't* feel peace. A very short, powerful sentence at the beginning of an earlier edition of *For the Strength of Youth* sums it up: "You cannot do wrong and feel right."[11] Personally, when I'm not living as I should, I know it—and so do you. I'm not talking about major sins, but minor mistakes. When I snap at someone, when I think ill of my neighbor, when I allow my thoughts to wander where they shouldn't, I don't feel as good. This is a testimony from the Spirit that the standards of the gospel are not just a set of random ideas but are rules of conduct based on truth, and that the Holy Ghost will not dwell in unclean places.

So should I commit a serious sin so that I can really feel the contrast? "God forbid" (see Paul's response to a similar question in Romans 6:1–2). But even when I sink into sin a little, or commit a minor sin, I feel it. I don't have to sink to the bottom of the ocean to know that it is wet! Latter-day Saint moviemaker Kieth Merrill put it beautifully:

> Righteousness brings happiness. Wickedness never does. If there were no God, no plan, no law, and no divine order, there would be no reason wickedness would not bring happiness. But it never does. The history of civilization is a testament that hedonism, perversion, brutality, corruption, and wickedness sow seeds of misery, sorrow, and destruction. It is not a quirk of evolution. It is evidence of a divinely appointed plan.[12]

When I served on a stake high council, I once had the privilege of being in a meeting where we were considering reinstating a young man who had been excommunicated but wanted to come back. He said something that I will never forget: "I finally decided that if I were to ever stop hurting, I had to start changing." Why was he hurting? He had been doing everything the world tells you is "fun": drinking and partying and breaking the law of chastity. But it didn't bring him happiness at all. Quite the contrary—he was miserable. If that kind of behavior is "fun," if that's the fun you're "missing out on," why would it hurt? But it *did* hurt, and he knew it. He felt it. He had learned for himself that *following the standards is the easiest way to live.*

"Wait a minute, Brother Bytheway! It is *not* easy to live the gospel!" you might be saying. Look again—I'm choosing my words carefully. I didn't say it was easy to live the gospel. I said it is the *easiest* way to live, because you avoid so many bad consequences. It's *easier* to live the standards than to suffer the dark, lonely, hollow feelings that come from not living them. This young man learned by experience and gained a personal witness that "wickedness never was happiness" (Alma 41:10).

As you know, they call that little standards book we carry around *For the Strength of Youth.* (If it had been up to me, I would have called it *How Not to Totally Mess Up Your Life,* but I wasn't on the committee.) When you view it this way, you can see that one of the nicest, kindest, most loving things our Father in Heaven has done is give us commandments. He is helping us avoid so many problems and their consequences by saying "Thou shalt not . . ." His commandments are not harsh and demanding, they are gentle and kind. That's why we sing the song, "How *gentle* God's commands! How *kind* his precepts are!"[13]

Feelings you experience as you live the gospel are often a witness of the Spirit. And the absence of those feelings when you stray from the gospel path is also evidence of the fruits of walking in the light.

So, How Do You Feel about These Feelings?

Is the burning in the bosom the only way to receive a witness of the Spirit? It certainly is not. The Lord is not limited in how He can communicate with us. Some people will discount feelings. They may say, "You can't trust your feelings!" Yes, feelings are not a perfect indicator, which is why feelings alone are not enough to base a testimony upon. Elder Bruce C. Hafen warned that "we may confuse lesser emotions with truly inspired impressions," and that "our feelings can sometimes be influenced by unwise people who would manipulate them."[14] So we have to be wise enough to sort out our feelings, to tell the difference between little whims and deep impressions, and to separate our feelings from our emotions. This ability comes with time and experience.

Feelings can take you on a roller-coaster ride, particularly when you're young. Teenagers experience quite a range of feelings, which is normal and expected. What we're talking about here are spiritual feelings, the kind you experience when you are quiet inside, when you are in spiritual places thinking about your life, your future, your identity, and other important and serious topics.

Pay attention to your feelings, especially when in spiritual environments. Notice how you feel at church, at seminary, while listening to general conference, or while reading your scriptures. You might feel the warm feeling in your heart, or you might feel joy, happiness, enlightenment, or peace. All these different feelings combine to become one of the "wires" feeding power to your dimmer switch.

Here's a note of caution—some may suffer from depression, and not just the "bad-hair day" type, but clinical depression, which is more biological than emotional and may require the help of professionals in medicine or psychology. When you're depressed, particularly if a doctor has prescribed some kind of medicine to help you deal with it, it can be harder to connect with the feelings we sometimes associate with testimony. Don't assume you have no testimony just because you can't "feel" it.

In addition to feelings, truth is verified in other ways. There are experiences, evidences, and logical conclusions. We probably speak most often of feelings, but the scriptures show that light comes from other sources as well. Next, we'll look at another important wire connected to our dimmer switch—we'll look at how our experiences can give us light and truth.

More LIGHT on the subject . . .

Voice of the Spirit video: http://www.mormonchannel.org/video/mormon-messages?v=910930358001

Receiving Revelation video: http://www.mormonchannel.org/power-of-the-holy-spirit?v=1365732854001

Notes

1. Boyd K. Packer, *That All May Be Edified* (Bookcraft, 1982), 335.

2. Dallin H. Oaks, "Teaching and Learning by the Spirit," *Ensign*, March 1997, 13.

3. Jay E. Jensen, "Have I Received an Answer from the Spirit?" *Ensign*, April 1989, 21–22.

4. Heber C. Kimball, in *Journal of Discourses*, 26 vols. (Latter-day Saints' Book Depot, 1854–1886), 4:222.

5. John H. Groberg, *Refuge and Reality* (Deseret Book, 2012), 3–4.

6. "Website ranks BYU as 7th happiest college," *Deseret News*, January 3, 2014.

7. Trent Toone, *No Excuses, No Regrets* (Deseret Book, 2013), 103.

8. Ibid., 105.

9. *The Teachings of Howard W. Hunter*, ed. Clyde J. Williams (Bookcraft, 1997), 184–85.

10. Personal correspondence from Bethany Sorenson.

11. *For the Strength of Youth* (The Church of Jesus Christ of Latter-day Saints, 1990), 4.

12. Kieth Merrill, in *Why I Believe* (Bookcraft, 2002), 230.

13. "How Gentle God's Commands," *Hymns* (The Church of Jesus Christ of Latter-day Saints, 1985), no. 125; emphasis added.

14. Bruce C. Hafen, *Spiritually Anchored in Unsettled Times* (Deseret Book, 2009), 61.

Wire Two: Experiences

Another "wire" or "power source" that feeds our dimmer switch of testimony is experience. The gospel of Jesus Christ is not only about knowing but about doing. If we *read* about the gospel, we're informed, but if we *practice* or *live* the gospel, we are transformed. This is a testimony of experience.

Go Jump in the Lake

Let's say you want to learn to swim. Here's one approach—you could go to the public library and check out every book they've got on swimming. You could sit in a nice, dry chair and read fifty volumes on the subject, including *Swimming for Dummies* and *Diving for Dolts*. Then you could go online. You could Google "swimming" and watch YouTube videos on diving, treading water, dog-paddling, and doing the backstroke. You could spend hours and hours researching and trying to absorb the essence of swimming. But let's face it, you haven't even gotten your feet wet. You've *read* a lot about swimming, but that's all. It's like trying to quench your thirst by drinking a glass of dehydrated water.

Now suppose your friend Bob, who cannot read, simply plugs his nose and jumps in the lake. He will know more in five seconds *by experience* than you do after hours and hours of research. You've read about swimming, but Bob has experienced it. He knows, by doing it, what swimming is all about on a completely different level from someone who has only read about it.

I Didn't Just Read about It, I Lived It!

We live in a world where many people who criticize the Church in books, articles, blog posts, and video clips have never even set foot inside one of our chapels! What do they know? My friend Brad Wilcox taught a group of youth:

Do you realize that just because you are here tonight, you know more about what happens in the Mormon church than many people who write books and make movies on the subject? Just because you are here tonight, just because you are an active member, do you realize that you are more of an expert about the Mormon church than many people who are asked questions about our faith on national television? Yes, you have testimonies of experience.[1]

A young man in my Book of Mormon class volunteered to give the opening prayer, and, as he got to his feet, I asked him to tell us a little about his life. Jonathan explained that he was a new convert. He had come into contact with the Church because of a girl he wanted to date. She invited him to several young single adult family home evening activities, until someone eventually persuaded him to listen to the missionaries. When his parents heard he was investigating the Church, they panicked! They Googled the Church and handed him a pile of anti-Mormon literature. He started reading it but eventually tossed it all in the trash because he knew *by experience* that it was false. The new friends he had made, the things he was learning, and the feelings he was experiencing had little relation to what he read from the Internet. What he knew by *experience* was more powerful than what had been written by critics of the Church. Someone once said, "A man with experience is never at the mercy of a man with an opinion."

Do in Order to *Know*

While doing research for this book, I read dozens of general conference talks on the topic of testimony. And practically every one of them referred to this very important saying of Jesus:

> If any man will do his will, he shall know of the doctrine, whether it be of God, or whether I speak of myself. (John 7:17)

Notice the heart of it—you must "do" in order to "know." Doing leads to experience; experience leads to knowing. "Doing" is a crucial part of the formula for gaining a testimony. Much of the world has this backwards. People say, "Once I know, then I'll do," or, "I want the benefit of a testimony, but I don't want to do any of the work." That's like standing in front of your fireplace and saying, "Give me heat, then I'll give you wood." We have another name for it—sign seeking: "If you will prove it to me, then I'll follow." But Jesus taught that we have to *do* the Lord's will in order to *know*, to gain a testimony of its truth. This is the difference between faith (believing) and faithfulness (action).

Former NFL quarterback Steve Young compared the experience of gaining a testimony to adjusting to playing football in the NFL. The game was so much faster than the college game that, instead of waiting to throw until he saw the open receiver, he learned he had to throw the ball with a little faith. He had to throw to where the receiver *should* be—in other words, he had to act before he knew:

> I do believe. I believe because I practiced my faith first without knowing and then felt the answers in my heart. Over time this faith produced conviction that I know more than anything else in my life, seen or unseen. I have felt God, I savor His written word, I love and listen to His ordained prophets, and He speaks to my heart.

. . . All you have to do is start "throwing the ball without seeing," and that faith will develop until you know that our Father in Heaven and His Son Jesus Christ live and are our hope individually and the hope for the whole world.[2]

Since we live in an "I'll believe it when I see it" world, we sometimes want the knowledge before we act, but knowledge of spiritual things doesn't come that way. President Dieter F. Uchtdorf observed, "Spiritual light rarely comes to those who merely sit in the darkness waiting for someone to flip a switch. It takes an act of faith to open our eyes to the light of Christ."[3]

Sincere Heart, Real Intent

As a missionary, you will want to help those you are teaching to gain testimonies. You will want them to *experience* the truth, not just hear it. You will try to persuade them to pray, to read the scriptures, and to participate in the Church in order to gain a testimony of experience. You will probably invite them to try Moroni's promise, to read and pray about the Book of Mormon. Many times in my Book of Mormon class, we have discussed what Moroni means when he invites readers to ask about the truthfulness of the Book of Mormon with both a "sincere heart" and "real intent." Are they the same thing? I don't think so. I think these two phrases emphasize the importance of both knowing and doing:

> And if ye shall ask with a sincere heart [I sincerely want to *know*], with real intent [I really intend to *do*], having faith in Christ, he will manifest the truth of it unto you, by the power of the Holy Ghost. (Moroni 10:4)

Once we take action, once we demonstrate our faith by taking a step into the unknown, God can become involved. President Marion G. Romney once remarked, "While the Lord will magnify us in both subtle and dramatic ways, he can only guide our footsteps when we move our feet."[4] Additionally, President Howard W. Hunter taught, "Action is one of the chief foundations of personal testimony. The surest witness is that which comes firsthand out of personal experience. . . . This, then, is the finest source of personal testimony. One knows because he has experienced."[5]

Young men reading this book will probably

recognize the principles we're talking about in the theme of the *Duty to God* program: "Learn, act, share" means to *learn* the doctrines of the gospel, then to *act* on them, and finally to *share* your experience and what you've become. In other words, if you will do His will (act), then you will know the doctrine (what you've learned will become a part of you) by experience.

Journal Entries over the Centuries

What are the scriptures? In many ways, the scriptures are testimonies of experiences. They are the journals of the house of Israel, recording how the Lord has dealt with them through the centuries and preserving their spiritual experiences. Someone once said, "Wise men learn by experience; super wise men learn from others' experience." The experiences of people in the scriptures "enlarge our memories" (see Alma 37:8), and our testimonies grow as we read their stories.

As a sixteen-year-old, I heard President Spencer W. Kimball plead with the members of the Church to keep a journal. I started it then, and I'm embarrassed to say I've stopped and started it many times, but it wasn't until more recently that I realized exactly *why* we should keep a journal. It's not only to keep track of our trips and trophies and triumphs. The main purpose is to catalog our spiritual experiences, or to document the Lord's hand in our lives. President Henry B. Eyring shared his purpose for writing in a journal (watch for the words "evidence" and "testimony"):

> Before I would write, I would ponder this question: "Have I seen the hand of God reaching out to touch us or our children or our family to-day?" As I kept at it, something began to happen. As I would cast my mind over the day, I would see evidence of what God had done for one of us that I had not recognized in the busy moments of the day. As that happened, and it happened often, I realized that trying to remember had allowed God to show me what He had done. More than gratitude began to grow in my heart. Testimony grew. I became ever more certain that our Heavenly Father hears and answers prayers.[6]

As we reread our journals, we recall the experiences that show us how the Lord is involved in our lives. As we count our blessings, gratitude and testimony will grow, "and it will surprise [us] what the Lord has done."[7]

A Bike and a Bus

My mission journal contains one particular "testimony of experience" that lights up my dimmer switch like a power surge. (I have to share a spiritual experience about me because I don't know any spiritual experiences about you.)

I was on a split with Elder Reidhead. We were cycling down Checkpoint Road, near Clark Air Force Base in Angeles City in the Philippines. As we were riding, a motorcycle pulled alongside and struggled to match our slow speed. The rider yelled through his helmet, "Anybody from Nevada?" We didn't normally encounter Americans in the Philippines, so it was kind of fun to speak with him. I hollered that we were from Utah and Arizona.

We conversed for a minute or two, and every time he twisted the accelerator, he'd zoom ahead of us, then coast until he slowed enough that we could talk. At one point when he zoomed ahead, I thought he had finished chatting with us and was about to turn left.

So I shouted, "See you later," and he stared at me as if to say, *Oh, you don't want to talk to me anymore? Fine.* Then he hit the accelerator with gusto, speeding straight ahead and out of sight. I felt terrible. I had thought he was finished talking to us, but evidently he wasn't, and without meaning to, I had just offended him. I felt ashamed, embarrassed, and about half an inch tall.

For two weeks, I pleaded with the Lord to let me meet that man again so that I could apologize and leave a better impression. But, to be honest, I didn't know how it could possibly happen. My chances of running into him were very small, since he wasn't in my area, and my area wasn't near the base. (I was in Elder Reidhead's area when I met him.) To make it more difficult, I really didn't know what he looked like. He'd had a helmet on, and all I could see were his eyes. Was his hair brown? Black? Blond? Did he have hair? I had no idea. I also heard there were thousands of Americans working at Clark Air Force Base. And even if I did see another American back in my area, how would I know if it was him? He would have to walk up to me and say, "I'm the guy you talked to on a motorcycle." Clearly, I needed a miracle. This was something only God could arrange.

A couple of weeks later, I was visiting the missionaries in a little town called Guagua, about forty-five minutes away from Angeles City. When our visit was over, we went to the bus station and checked the schedule. It appeared we had just missed the bus, but then we saw it pull around the corner. The bus appeared to be full of people, and we walked down the aisle looking for a seat. The only available seats were in the back, which were the worst seats of all because of the noise and heat produced by the engine. There were four American servicemen in the back next to the only empty seats. We would normally have chosen to sit by Filipinos since the American military branches were out of our area, but in this instance, we sat by the servicemen because that was the only available space on the bus.

Suddenly, one of the Americans broke the silence and confronted us with, "The only thing I want to know is why you guys don't serve in the military." I explained that he had us confused with another religious group, and that Latter-day Saints did serve in the military. I mentioned a few members I knew on the base. Just then, another one of the Americans leaned forward and said, "I talked to a couple of you guys the other day."

Startled, I blurted out, "Were you by any chance on a motorcycle?"

"Yeah," he said.

My jaw dropped a bit, and I blubbered, "That was you?" Amazingly, this was the same man!

Every time I recall this story, I'm amazed all over again. Not only did the Lord arrange for us to meet, but He arranged that the only empty seats on the bus would be next to the man I was looking for and that we would have forty-five minutes to talk. And we did! I would love to tell you he joined the Church, but the fact is, he wasn't the least bit interested. I'm sure the Lord knew that, too, yet He answered my prayer in a dramatic fashion. I had the opportunity to leave a much better impression about the Church and the missionaries in that man's mind.

I learned *by experience* that the Lord can get two people in the same place at the same time. (Later in my life, this knowledge increased my faith that the

Lord could also help me find someone to marry.) I also learned in a powerful way that He can answer prayers.

I could share a dozen other such stories, but these are only *my* experiences. For your testimony to grow, you must catalog your own experiences. Again, that is the principal reason for keeping a journal. When we sense the Lord's involvement in our lives, our testimony grows. Elder Gerald N. Lund calls these events "divine signatures," because we detect the hand of the Lord guiding us or directing our experiences. They've also been referred to as "tender mercies." What experiences have you had that have strengthened your testimony? Make sure you catalog these events, and if you ever feel your light growing dim, take your journal off the shelf so that you can *read* and *remember*.

Happily, you have a lifetime of experiences ahead of you, a lifetime of opportunities to "do His will" so that you may "know of the doctrine." Notice how the Lord connects obedience to *light* and to *knowing* in this verse: "He that keepeth his commandments receiveth truth and light, until he is glorified in truth and knoweth all things" (D&C 93:28). Yup, you've got to live it to know it.

So far, we've talked about feelings and experiences that have given added light to our testimony. But there's more! Next, we'll talk about evidence.

More LIGHT on the subject . . .

Sister Bonnie L. Oscarson:
https://www.lds.org/general-conference
/2013/10/be-ye-converted?lang=eng

Elder David A. Bednar:
https://www.lds.org/general
-conference/2005/04/the-tender
-mercies-of-the-lord?lang=eng

Gerald N. Lund, *Divine Signatures* (Deseret Book, 2011).

Notes

1. Brad Wilcox, *Filling Your Testimony Tank*, talk on CD (Deseret Book, 1999).
2. Steve Young, in *Why I Believe* (Bookcraft, 2002), 340–41.
3. Dieter F. Uchtdorf, "The Hope of God's Light," *Ensign*, May 2013, 75.

4. Marion G. Romney, "The Basic Principles of Church Welfare," *Ensign*, May 1981, 91.

5. Howard W. Hunter, in Conference Report, April 1967, 116.

6. Henry B. Eyring, "O Remember, Remember," *Ensign*, November 2007, 67.

7. "Count Your Blessings," *Hymns* (The Church of Jesus Christ of Latter-day Saints, 1985), no. 241.

Wire Three: Evidences

Sariah had a testimony that Lehi was directed by God to leave Jerusalem. How did she get it? Did she feel a burning feeling? Did she feel peace or clarity? How did she come to know? Sariah had complained against Lehi, saying that he was a visionary man and had led them away in the wilderness, and that her sons were "no more." But when the boys came over the hill, safe and sound and carrying the plates of brass, suddenly she knew. It was evidence to her. In Sariah's words:

> *Now I know* of a surety that the Lord hath commanded my husband to flee into the wilderness; yea, and *I also know* of a surety that the Lord

hath protected my sons, and delivered them out
of the hands of Laban. (1 Nephi 5:8; emphasis
added)

We might conclude that Sariah's testimony that
her husband, Lehi, was a prophet came primarily from
evidence. Her prayers were answered! We use evidence
to prove something. But we can't really prove the
gospel is true, can we? No. Eventually, we are backed
up to the wall of faith, and the Lord designed it that
way. In fact, one of the strengths of our missionary effort is that we do not tell people, "Just take my word
for it." More often, we say just the opposite—"*Don't*
take my word for it—go find out for yourself."

So why talk about evidence? It's only one of the
wires leading to our dimmer switch, but it is important because it creates an environment for suspending
disbelief. Evidence can move people up a notch on the
dimmer switch from "I doubt" to "I wonder." The Book
of Mormon missionary duo of Nephi and Lehi, who
were both sons of Helaman,

did minister unto the people, declaring throughout all the regions round about all the things
which they had heard and seen, insomuch that

the more part of the Lamanites were convinced of them, because of the *greatness of the evidences* which they had received. (Helaman 5:50; emphasis added)

For those of us who already believe, finding new evidence is reassuring. (And really fun!) Some might consider their feelings and experiences as evidence, and yes, that's a fair use of the word. Feelings, experiences, and evidences may overlap a bit, but I'm going to use the term *evidence* mostly to refer to things that verify the truth of the scriptures and of prophecies.

The Book of Mormon

When the Book of Mormon was first published, critics immediately attacked its truthfulness because of some of the descriptions it gave of ancient life. For example, it spoke of cement in the ancient world. "There was no cement back then," they said. But years went by, and they found evidence of ancient cement. Others criticized it because it spoke of horses, and they said there weren't any horses here back then. Then they found some. Then they said there were no elephants. Then they found some. They also said there was no barley here before Columbus. Then they found some.

If Joseph Smith had written the Book of Mormon, and if he had consulted the scientists of the day, he would not have included things like cement, horses, elephants, and barley. But he didn't write the Book of Mormon. He translated it. And what were thought to be weaknesses of the Book of Mormon are now strengths that provide evidence it is true!

There are evidences in *what* the book says, but also in *the way* the book is written. One of the most interesting of these evidences is *chiasmus*. Back in the 1960s, Elder John W. Welch was a twenty-year-old missionary in Germany. He and his companion chose to spend one P-day attending a lecture in a Catholic church about something called "chiasmus"—a complex form of Hebrew writing and structure in the New Testament.

Elder Welch was fascinated by the lecture and appreciated what it taught him about understanding the Bible. One morning, Elder Welch woke up early with a prompting and an interesting thought—could there be chiasmus in the Book of Mormon? After all, the people who wrote the Book of Mormon came out of Jerusalem, so perhaps their Hebrew culture influenced the way they wrote the book.

So Elder Welch searched, and he found chiasmus or "chiastic" structures in the Book of Mormon. He found *many* of them, and he published an article about them in the February 1972 *New Era* magazine while he was a doctoral student at Oxford. The article is titled, "Chiasmus in the Book of Mormon, or the Book of Mormon Does It Again."

The current Book of Mormon institute manual describes chiasmus like this:

> Chiasmus, sometimes called an inverted parallelism, is a Hebrew literary form where words or ideas are arranged in a certain order and then repeated in reverse order. This repetition emphasizes important ideas and words. In addition, the writer's main idea is often located at the center of the chiasmus. Alma used chiasmus to tell the story of his conversion to his son Helaman. The presence of Semitic literary forms such as chiasmus in the Book of Mormon is an external witness that the book is what the

Prophet Joseph Smith taught that it is: a translation of an ancient text written in a Middle Eastern language.[1]

So what is an example of a chiasmus? Here's a short one:

A. It's *nice*
    B. to be *important*,
    B. but it's more *important*
A. to be *nice.*

We used the words *nice* and *important* and then repeated them in reverse order, *important* and *nice*.

Here's the first chiasmus John Welch discovered from King Benjamin's speech (Mosiah 5:10–12):

A. whosoever shall not take upon him the NAME of Christ
    B. must be CALLED by some other name;
        C. therefore, he findeth himself on the LEFT HAND of God.
            D. And I would that ye should REMEMBER also, that this is the NAME
                E. that I said I should give unto you that never should be BLOTTED OUT,
                    F. except it be through TRANSGRESSION;

> F. therefore, take heed that ye do not
> TRANSGRESS,
> E. that the name be not BLOTTED OUT of your
> hearts.
> D. I say unto you, I would that ye should REMEMBER
> to retain the NAME
> C. written always in your hearts, that ye are not found on
> the LEFT HAND of God,
> B. but that ye hear and know the voice by which ye shall be
> CALLED,
> A. and also, the NAME by which he shall call you.

Perhaps the most amazing occurrence of chiasmus in the Book of Mormon appears in Alma 36. What verses, you ask? *All of them*. The entire chapter is a huge chiasmus, a masterpiece! And what is the pivot point, or the main idea at the center? It's Jesus Christ. This was not an accident. It's an intricate piece of writing, and yet Joseph Smith never mentioned it. It was, and is, evidence that the Book of Mormon is of ancient origin, and it was hidden in plain sight for many, many decades.

See if you can find another example of chiasmus in Mosiah 3:18–19. (Hint: find the word *humble* in both verses, then find *child* and *children*, and look for other

Alma 36

A. Give ear to my words (v. 1)

 B. Keep the commandments of God, and ye shall prosper in the land (v. 1)

  C. Do as I have done (v. 2)

   D. Remember the captivity of our fathers, for they were in bondage (v. 2)

    E. He surely did deliver them (v. 2)

     F. Trust in God (v. 3)

      G. Supported in their trials, and their troubles, and their afflictions (v. 3)

       H. I would not that ye think that I know of myself—but of God (v. 4)

        I. Born of God (v. 5)

         J. I went about seeking to destroy the church of God (v. 6)

          K. Neither had I the use of my limbs (v. 10)

           L. I thought that I might not be brought to the presence of my God (v. 15)

            M. The pains of a damned soul (v. 16)

             N. Harrowed up by the memory of my many sins (v. 17)

              O. I remembered one JESUS CHRIST, a Son of God (v. 17)

              O. I cried within my heart: O JESUS, thou Son of God (v. 18)

             N. Harrowed up by the memory of my sins no more (v. 19)

            M. Joy as exceeding as was my pain (v. 20)

           L. My soul did long to be there (in the presence of God) (v. 22)

          K. My limbs received strength again (v. 23)

         J. I labored to bring souls to repentance (v. 24)

        I. Born of God (v. 26)

       H. My knowledge is of God (v. 26)

      G. Supported under trials, troubles, and afflictions (v. 27)

     F. Trust in him (v. 27)

    E. He has delivered them out of bondage and captivity (v. 28)

   D. Retain a remembrance of their captivity (v. 29)

  C. Know as I do know (v. 30)

 B. Keep the commandments of God, and ye shall prosper (v. 30)

A. This according to his word (v. 30)

matching words or ideas as you work toward the center.) Again, Book of Mormon chiasmus was discovered by a young missionary. It had been there all along, right there on the surface, but an inspired young man noticed it and "brought it to light." Which brings up an interesting question—what evidences might you discover in your lifetime?

To read Brother Welch's article, go to http://www.lds.org/new-era/1972/02/ chiasmus-in-the-book-of-mormon?lang=eng

A Fingerprint of Words

Another evidence of the Book of Mormon comes from a science called wordprints. Each person writes and uses words in his or her own individual way—a way so unique that the person's writing creates a "wordprint." Just as fingerprints identify an individual, wordprints provide a way to identify the author of a written work. Wordprints have been used to identify the authors of anonymous works and also to catch criminals.

Using the science of wordprints, the letters and

writings of Joseph Smith could be tested against the Book of Mormon to see if they were written by the same author. Wordprints could also reveal if the book had more than one author.

Researchers, some of whom were not Latter-day Saints, concluded that it was "statistically indefensible" to suggest that the Book of Mormon was written by Joseph Smith or Oliver Cowdery. Furthermore, they showed that the Book of Mormon was written by multiple authors.

For more on wordprint studies, visit:
http://davies-linguistics.byu.edu/ling485
/for_class/30.3Hilton.pdf

Nahom and Bountiful

Another interesting evidence supporting the Book of Mormon involves Nahom, a place on the Arabian Peninsula. You'll recall that while on their journey out of Jerusalem, Ishmael died in a place "which was called Nahom" (1 Nephi 16:34). Other stops along their route were named by Lehi, like the "Valley of

Lemuel," and so forth, but this place, Nahom, already had a name. Can we find evidence that such a place really existed, and did it exist around 600 B.C., when Lehi and his family were on their journey?

Remarkably (but not surprisingly to those of us who believe), there is such a place. And it is exactly where it ought to be, and it existed at the time Lehi and his caravan would have passed through. Critics might suggest that Joseph Smith must have gone down to the local public library and found a map of the ancient Middle East showing a place called Nahom, but no such map existed in the United States at the time. Since then, maps have been found verifying the existence of the place called Nahom.

After Ishmael was buried in Nahom, the family traveled "nearly eastward" from that time forth until they reached a land they called "Bountiful." Why would they call it Bountiful? "Because of its much fruit" (1 Nephi 17:1, 5). Critics of the Book of Mormon scoffed at the suggestion that there was a place on the Arabian Peninsula with fresh water, sufficient timber to build a ship, and a bounty of fruit. But we now know that there are a few candidates for Nephi's land of

Bountiful, one of which is Wadi Sayq in the kingdom of Oman.

If you look on Google Earth, it's quite startling to see a tiny oasis of green on the southern edge of countless square miles of desert. But there it is, directly east of ancient Nahom, with fresh water, trees, and fruit (probably meaning dates), just as the Book of Mormon suggests.

More could be said about each of these evidences we've discussed, and you can find more by visiting some of the sources listed at the end of this chapter.

We've Known That for Years

This headline appeared on *USA Today's* website: "Earthshaking news: There may be other planets like ours." The article began with this stunning pronouncement: "We are not alone. There are likely 'tens of billions' of Earth-like planets in our Milky Way galaxy, according to a study released Monday by astronomers. . . ." (*USA Today,* November 4, 2013).

Wow, they could have knocked me over with a feather. Sometimes it takes a long time for science to catch up with revelation. Along with the Restoration came additional ancient scripture, such as the Pearl of Great Price. Did ancient prophets know about other planets? Yes. The Lord told Moses, "And worlds without number have I created" (Moses 1:33), and Enoch said to the Lord, "Were it possible that man could number the particles of the earth, yea, millions of earths like this, it would not be a beginning to the number of thy creations" (Moses 7:30). The folks at USA Today were rattled by the news, but we've known it for years.

Prophecies

Suppose some teenager sat next to you on a bus, tapped you on the shoulder, and said, "A hundred years from now, people will still be talking about me. In fact, people of every nation, every race, and every language will be talking about me." You'd probably question his sanity, zip up your backpack, and move to a new seat.

Consider Joseph Smith, who claimed he was visited by an angel named Moroni. And what did Moroni tell him? "He called me by name," Joseph said, and explained that "my name should be had for good and evil among all nations, kindreds, and tongues, or that it should be both good and evil spoken of among all people" (Joseph Smith–History 1:33).

And what do we see today? Missionaries all over the world, teaching people about Joseph Smith's first prayer. Some accept it, some do not, but Moroni's words have come true. People among all nations, kindreds, and tongues are encountering the story of the Restoration. Just remember that if you ever hear someone being critical of Joseph Smith, they are giving you evidence. They are fulfilling a prophecy made by Moroni.

What else did Joseph Smith say? When I was called on my mission, there were about three million members of the Church. Today, there are nearly five times that many members! My parents used to tell me that temples would "dot the earth." When I was on my mission, we used a flip chart, a book of illustrations, to help us present our lessons. We had a photo in our flip chart with all sixteen temples, and I could name them all. How many temples are there today? I don't know, what time is it? I believe there are about 140, half of them with names I cannot pronounce, and by the time this book comes off the presses, the number will be even higher.

Have you ever seen the movie showing a map of

the earth and the organization of new stakes around the world? (See the link below). It always reminds me of what Joseph Smith said to a group of Saints:

> Brethren I have been very much edified and instructed in your testimonies here tonight, but I want to say to you before the Lord, that you know no more concerning the destinies of this Church and kingdom than a babe upon its mother's lap. You don't comprehend it. . . . It is only a little handfull of Priesthood you see here tonight, but this Church will fill North and South America—it will fill the world.[2]

The growth of the Church is a fulfillment of prophecy and an evidence of its truthfulness. If you watch the movie, you will begin to see how the Church is filling North and South America. You'll also see that we have a lot of work to do in order to "fill the world" (that's where you come in).

https://www.lds.org/media-library /video/2010-07-060-the-gospel -shall-roll-forth

Trees and Fruit

Jesus spoke of evidence when He taught how to recognize false prophets: "Ye shall know them by their fruits" (Matthew 7:16). In other words, in order to *know*, look at the *results*. The fruits and the results are evidence.

If you plant an apple seed, how long will it take before you get your first apple? It actually may take four to six years or even longer. Similarly, seeing the fruits of the gospel may take time, but eventually, those seeds produce evidence. If it's good fruit, then you also know it is a good tree, since "A good tree cannot bring forth evil fruit, neither can a corrupt tree bring forth good fruit" (Matthew 7:18).

What does the gospel do for people? How are they changed? How do they grow? What do they become? If we were to live what the gospel teaches for many years, then what would we expect the fruits of time spent in study, self-control, service, and standards to be? (For the sake of contrast, what would you expect the fruits to be of a life spent in drugs, pornography, alcohol, and unchastity?)

The *teachings* of the gospel are what we *know*. The

fruits of the gospel are what we *become*. You'll remember that the stripling warriors were described as young men who "were true at all times" (Alma 53:20). It doesn't say they *knew* the truth at all times, but they *were* true. This is something beyond just knowing what's right. When we live what we know, we *become* true. The thirteenth article of faith begins by saying, "We believe in being honest, true . . ." Why doesn't it just say, "We believe in honesty and truth"? The key word in there is *being*—*being* honest, *being* true. It's not just about knowing things, it's about *being* something, or, in other words, *becoming* something.

Look around you. Look at the people you most admire. Look at your grandparents. Look at the faithful members of your ward. Look at the leaders of our Church. What has the gospel helped these people become? Look at the evidence! Know them by their fruits.

I am blessed to have met hundreds of teenagers around the Church. They are wonderful! Happy, energetic, curious, faithful, and smart. They have their problems, too, which is part of life on this fallen planet, but through all the bumps in the road, they are headed in the right direction, and the goodness of their lives is evidence of the truth of the gospel. Robert F. Bennett, a former United States senator, spoke of the fruits of the gospel enjoyed by Latter-day Saint teenagers when he reported:

> Our daughter told me of a high school teacher in California where our grandson was enrolled who knew all about all of her students: which ones were on drugs, which ones were caught up in messy sexual relationships, and which ones were drinking too much. This teacher told our daughter that our grandson had none of these problems; indeed, she said, "*All* the Mormon kids in my class are just fine."[3]

Jesus made this interesting statement: "And ye shall know the truth, and the truth shall make you free" (John 8:32). We may well ask, "Free from what?" Among other things, you'll be free from addictions to drugs or alcohol, free from having "messy sexual relationships" and all the associated heartache—in a nutshell, free from the bitter fruits of living like the world. I don't want to make a list, but how many Hollywood celebrities, even teenage pop stars, who appear to "have it all"—fame, money, and popularity—proceed to make a train wreck of their lives? You can name names, no doubt. Forgive my informal language, but dude, when even the *tabloids* have no respect for you, that's bad.

Latter-day Saints have problems too; we're not all perfect. No doubt some LDS teens might be struggling with the problems mentioned above. But we're not talking about individual teenagers here. We're talking about examining the fruits of the *gospel*. And when people live the *gospel*, no matter their age, they enjoy the fruits. And those fruits are evidence of the gospel's goodness and its truth.

Our Invitation to the World: "Consider Our Evidence"

In addition to having feelings and experiences to strengthen our testimonies, we have evidence. Can we prove the Church is true using evidence alone? No, but we can testify of the evidences, just as Peter and John did: "For we cannot but speak the things which we have *seen* and *heard*" (Acts 4:20; emphasis added).

In addition, Jesus taught that we could know something is good or true by examining its fruits.

Our Church is not just another take on Christianity or another way to interpret the Bible. The Restoration brought with it something else: 531 pages of something else. Perhaps our greatest piece of evidence that the gospel has been restored is the Book of Mormon. *Preach My Gospel* teaches that while God has continually reached out to His people on the earth, people have continually rejected Him. But, following the same pattern, God has reached out again in our day. Watch for the word *evidence* twice in this paragraph:

> Our invitation to you and all people is to add to the truths you already treasure. Consider our evidence that our Heavenly Father and His Son, Jesus Christ, have again reached out to God's children in love and revealed the fulness of the gospel to a prophet. This prophet's name is Joseph Smith. The evidence of this glorious truth is found in a book—the Book of Mormon—which you can read, ponder, and pray about. If you pray with a sincere heart, with real

intent and faith in Christ, God will tell you by the power of the Holy Ghost that it is true.[4]

Entire books have been written about evidences, and this is only one chapter in one short book. Many other evidences could be mentioned, but I've chosen only a few that are interesting and compelling to me. It is just nice to know that the evidences are there, and that if you continue to search, you will continue to find, and more power and illumination will result.

More LIGHT on the subject . . .

Elder Jeffrey R. Holland: https://www.lds.org/general-conference/2009/10/safety-for-the-soul?lang=eng#10-PD50019113_000_030

Daniel Peterson, "A Scholar Looks at Evidences for the Book of Mormon," http://www.youtube.com/watch?v=VV8QN7bIeEE

John Hilton III, *The Little Book of Book of Mormon Evidences* (Deseret Book, 2007).

Notes

1. *Book of Mormon Student Manual, Religion 121–122* (The Church of Jesus Christ of Latter-day Saints, 2009), 232.

2. Joseph Smith, as quoted by Wilford Woodruff in Conference Report, April 1898, 57.

3. Robert F. Bennett, in *Why I'm a Mormon,* ed. Joseph A. Cannon (Ensign Peak, 2012), 28.

4. *Preach My Gospel* (The Church of Jesus Christ of Latter-day Saints, 2004), 41.

Wire Four: Logic

We've discussed Feelings, Experiences, Evidences, and now we'll look at the "L" in F.E.E.L. I've chosen to call it "Logic," but we might just as well call it "Reason." (But that would make my acronym F.E.E.R., and I didn't like the sound of that.) On my mission, one of the phrases I heard many times from investigators as we taught them the gospel was, "This makes sense." Something clicked in their heads, and our message felt logical to them. For some people, the "Logic" component makes a big difference and is a large source of their light. I once heard someone refer to those who really prefer evidence and logic to hold onto as "Iron Rodders," and those who were more "feelings" oriented as "Liahonas." What's nice is that we can be a little of both!

Interestingly, the Lord said, "Yea, behold, I will tell you in your mind *and* in your heart" (D&C 8:2; emphasis added). So gaining a testimony is not a mindless exercise, and it isn't heartless, either. That's why, in this little book, I've divided the sources of light into four parts, but you could also divide them up like this:

In your mind:	In your heart:
Evidences	Feelings
Logic	Experiences

So, let's talk about the logic or the reason involved in strengthening our testimony. A few of the things that "click" logically for me will be the subject of this chapter, but you can always make your own list, and I really hope you will.

The Restoration

Can you imagine this conversation?

Power Company: Hello, Tri-State Power, I'm Doof N. Schmirtz, may I help you?

Caller: Yes, could you restore my power?

Power Company: Oh, is your power out?

Caller: No.

Power Company: Oh. So your lights are on?

Caller: Yes.

Power Company: Okay, um, but you're asking me to restore your power with my *Restorinator?*

Caller: Yes.

Power Company: But your power is on, and our computers show that there are no outages in the *entire Tri-State Area!*

You wouldn't call the power company and ask them to restore your power if you never lost it, right? We use a word very often in the Church, and we should. The word is *restoration.* But the word *restoration* itself is like "part two" of a two-part story. It implies that something was lost that later had to be restored. In this context, we have another word for *lost,* and that word is *apostasy.* An apostasy is a "falling away," or, to put it even stronger, a mutiny.

You've probably already learned in seminary about the Great Apostasy. After Jesus was crucified, the

Apostles went into all the world to teach the gospel. They were treated horribly, and, according to tradition, all of them met violent deaths (except for John the Revelator, who escaped). Eventually, the Lord withdrew the priesthood from the earth. What happened to the church that the Savior organized? Brother Robert J. Matthews explained:

> During the second century the leadership of the church changed from the Apostles to the Greek Fathers, but the actual transmission is shrouded in mystery. It is as if a busload of people had headed up Provo Canyon with a certain destination in mind and with a well-defined map. In the canyon they encountered a heavy fog. During the fog the bus made an unscheduled stop. New passengers got on board. There was a struggle. When the bus emerged from the fog, the bus held new drivers and some new passengers and was following a different map and contemplating a different destination. The new drivers were heavily influenced by Greek philosophy. This was not a gentle drifting away.[1]

Sometime after the deaths of the Apostles and before the formation of the Catholic church, something happened. Things that were "plain and most precious; and also many covenants" were altered or taken away (1 Nephi 13:26). Some scholars refer to this as the "hellenization" of Christianity. *Hellenization* refers to the infusion of Greek culture and philosophy, the impact of which is still evident today.

President Boyd K. Packer taught that good people remained, but the Church and the keys and priesthood to lead it were gone (be sure to notice the references to light and dark):

> The Twelve established the Church of Jesus Christ; and despite persecution, it flourished. But as the centuries passed, the flame flickered and dimmed. Ordinances were changed or abandoned. The line was broken, and the authority to confer the Holy Ghost as a gift was gone. The Dark Ages of apostasy settled over the world. But always, as it had from the beginning, the Spirit of God inspired worthy souls. We owe an immense debt to the protestors and the reformers who preserved the scriptures and translated them. They

knew something had been lost. They kept the flame alive as best they could. Many of them were martyrs. But protesting was not enough; nor could reformers restore that which was gone. In time, a great diversity of churches arose. When all was prepared, the Father and the Son appeared to the boy Joseph in the Grove, and those words spoken at the river Jordan were heard once again, "This is My Beloved Son. Hear Him!"[2]

Just as the Fall of man required an Atonement to make things right, the "fall" or apostasy of the Church required a Restoration.

While Appeared Two Heavenly Beings . . .

When the Prophet Joseph Smith saw the Father and the Son in the Sacred Grove, he instantly learned things about the nature of God that had been lost, changed, or enshrouded in mystery in the centuries after Christ walked the earth. Joseph Smith declared, "Could you gaze into heaven five minutes, you would know more than you would by reading all that ever was written on the subject."[3]

In your interactions with friends of other faiths,

you may have encountered some who say we Mormons are not Christian because we don't accept the doctrine of the Trinity. Our first article of faith states, "We believe in God, the Eternal Father, and in His Son, Jesus Christ, and in the Holy Ghost." So we believe very strongly in the Father, Son, and Holy Ghost, but we also believe that they are "one" in purpose, not in substance. Jesus described the type of oneness He enjoys with the Father when He prayed to the Father for His believers, "That they all may be one; as thou, Father, art in me, and I in thee, that they also may be one in us" (John 17:21).

If people were to come from another planet and read the Bible, I doubt very much that they would come up with the doctrine of the Trinity. The idea of the Trinity was a product of many postbiblical councils attempting to harmonize what was written in the Bible with the learning of Greek philosophy. The creeds that attempt to describe the Trinity use heavy philosophical terms, language unlike anything in the Bible itself. Words like *consubstantial*, *uncreate*, and *trinity* are not biblical; they were an attempt to make the Christian beliefs acceptable to Greek intellectuals.

My testimony is strengthened as I learn the true nature of God as revealed in the Restoration. That truth makes sense to me and restores Him as literally my "Father in Heaven," not just an indefinable, incomprehensible, spirit mass. This is a complex subject, but a very interesting one that will help your testimony if you're willing to do some more research. If you'd like a more detailed discussion, I'll refer you to how Elder Dallin H. Oaks and Elder Jeffrey R. Holland approached it in the following general conference addresses:

Elder Dallin H. Oaks:
http://www.lds.org/general
-conference/1995/04/apostasy
-and-restoration?lang=eng

Elder Jeffrey R. Holland:
http://www.lds.org/general-conference
/2007/10/the-only-true-god-and
-jesus-christ-whom-he-hath
-sent?lang=eng

You might also read the brief discussion of "The Great Apostasy" in *Preach My Gospel*, pages 36–37.

Crusades and Inquisitions

The Crusades were attempts by the medieval church to take Jerusalem from non-Christians by military force. Resentments for the killing of Muslims to retake the Holy Land still exist today. The inquisitions were trials to discover if people were secretly engaging in "heresy," such as embracing Protestantism or following their former religions. Many were tortured in horrible, unspeakable ways until they confessed. These inquisitions continued for centuries. It doesn't make sense to me that the Savior or His church would torture people until they confessed.

Modern critics of Christianity will say, "Christianity has caused more wars than any other movement," and they may be right. People still do terrible things in the name of God. But logic and reason tell me that is not what Christianity did to man—it is what man did to Christianity. The fruits of apostate Christianity were often bitter. Brother Kieth Merrill put it strongly:

> Traditional Christianity is tarnished by an unholy history of apostasy, corruption, and horrific campaigns of violence carried out in the

shadow of the cross. The Church of Jesus Christ of Latter-day Saints is the only Christian church that escapes the disturbing legacy of power, politics, and perversions during the Dark Ages.[4]

Please don't misunderstand. Do other churches have goodness and truth? Absolutely. I have seen it personally, and I've been humbled by the devotion to Christ exhibited by many members of other faiths. The Prophet Joseph Smith taught, "We don't ask any people to throw away any good they have got; we only ask them to come and get more."[5] President Gordon B. Hinckley made a similar statement: "Let me say that we appreciate the truth in all churches and the good which they do. We say to the people, in effect, you bring with you all the good that you have, and then let us see if we can add to it."[6]

Nevertheless, there was in fact an Apostasy that was foretold by the prophets in numerous scriptures. The Apostasy was severe enough that it required a Restoration—a reformation was not sufficient. When the sons and daughters of God drift away from the teachings of Jesus, bad things happen. To me, this is just more evidence of the Apostasy and of the need for a Restoration.

The Book of Mormon

The Book of Mormon is another testament of Jesus Christ, from a different part of the world than the Bible. It makes logical sense to me that the Savior would visit His "other sheep," and that they would hear *His voice* (John 10:16), just as the Bible says. The Title Page of the Book of Mormon declares that the book's purpose is to convince "Jew and Gentile that Jesus is the Christ, the Eternal God, manifesting himself unto all nations." Look at those last two words, *all nations*. Yes, we have the Book of Mormon, but if the others Jesus visited also kept records, one day we'll have even more witnesses of Jesus Christ. Wouldn't that be wonderful? It would, because we have only a fraction of what Jesus taught. The very last verse in the book of John says:

And there are also many other things which Jesus did, the which, if they should be written every one, I suppose that even the world itself could not contain the books that should be written. Amen. (John 21:25)

Can you imagine that? The world couldn't contain the books? So maybe four years of seminary won't be enough when more of these books come forth. Isn't it exciting to think about? Perhaps in the Millennium we won't have triple combinations and quads, maybe we'll have pentabooks and septabooks and octabooks or more. Thank heavens for iPads and tablets with gigabytes of memory! Not only is it exciting to think of more records coming forth, it's logical—it makes sense.

Could Any Man Write This Book?

Having written a few books in my time, and knowing the difficulty of the process, I add my testimony to those of so many others who have said the same thing—there is no way that Joseph Smith could have written the Book of Mormon.

At one time, Elder David A. Bednar was a university professor, and he wrote a 650-page book with another professor over a two-year period. When Elder Bednar opened the first box of brand-new books, he asked himself a question:

"Why did you write this book?" When you really think about it, investing so much time and effort in a project that so quickly becomes obsolete is rather foolish. As I posed the question to myself and as I was pondering, the thought came to me, "Because now you know by experience that Joseph Smith could not have written the Book of Mormon." . . . With eight years of university training, with two years of very dedicated work, with an editorial staff, with personal computers, with spell checkers and thesauruses online, with the Internet and the other resources that are so readily available, when I picked up the book that I had written and opened it up, I still found mistakes. And within a matter of twelve months, this book upon which I had worked so hard and so long was obsolete and had to be revised. Brothers and sisters, you could take a team of the brightest people on the earth, as large a team as you might want, with all of the support staff, all of the computer technology, and all of the assistance that you can imagine, and such a team could not produce one page of a Book of Mormon.[7]

This testimony of the Book of Mormon is based on a logical conclusion. You may come to the same conclusion yourself. I hope that someday you will have the opportunity to write a book, or a master's thesis, a doctoral dissertation, or even just a long research paper. You will begin to appreciate what it would take to write the Book of Mormon.

Having Faith and Being Faithful

Our Church requires a lot of us—a lot of time on Sundays, and a lot of time during the week doing service projects, home teaching, visiting teaching, mourning with those who mourn, comforting those who stand in need of comfort (see Mosiah 18:9), and a million other things.

Some LDS teenagers are told by their friends that we believe our "works," or our righteous acts, will save us, and therefore, we are discounting the Atonement and the need for Christ. They might even claim we are not Christian because of our emphasis on good works. They misunderstand our doctrine. We are "all beggars," as King Benjamin said (Mosiah 4:19), and none of us can "earn" or demand our salvation. The Book of Mormon teaches that we must rely "alone" and "wholly" upon the merits of Christ (Moroni

6:4; 2 Nephi 31:19). His is the only name given under heaven whereby all mankind may be saved (see 2 Nephi 31:21). Nevertheless, the Lord who "went about doing good" (Acts 10:38) tells us to "Be not weary in well-doing" (D&C 64:33).

One time, while visiting another state, I was handed a tract that told me all I had to do to be saved was "Accept Jesus as my personal Savior." It even gave me the exact words to say. That was it! Well, Jesus Christ is absolutely my Savior and my only hope for salvation. But it doesn't make sense to me that simply saying a sentence is what Jesus is asking us to do, or what He asked His disciples in the Bible to do.

We *believe* in Christ, but we *follow* Christ in order to *become* like Christ. When the rich ruler came to Jesus and asked, "What must I do to have eternal life?" Jesus did NOT say, "Just say this sentence, and you're pretty much saved." He told him to keep the commandments, give all his wealth to the poor, and follow Him! (see Luke 18:18–23). And that's what we're trying to do, to follow Him. Of course, all the good works we could do will never be enough to save us. We need a Savior for that. We are never going to be perfect in this life, and Jesus knows that. That's why we ask Him to forgive us of our sins and change our hearts—to do for us what we cannot do for ourselves. But we can strive to follow Christ, and there is great growth in striving. It's part of "becoming." I believe the Savior loves us so much, He's going to ask difficult things of us so that we can grow and develop. That makes sense to me too.

My friend Brad Wilcox tells the story of a newly baptized young man who traveled to another city to participate in an all-state band. While getting ready for bed in their hotel, some of the boys in his room began talking about things they had done.

> I didn't like what they were saying, so I pretended to be asleep, but I heard them bragging about the drugs that they were taking. One guy was even selling drugs in an elementary school. They spoke of the shoplifting they had gotten away with and the young women they had defiled. Suddenly, one of the guys threw a pillow at me and said, "Hey, I heard you joined the Mormon Church." I said, "Yeah, what about it?" He said, "My minister says you are going to hell."

I don't know a lot about the Church—I mean,
I don't know the scriptures or the doctrine very
well. But one thing I know for sure is that there
is no way that those guys can be talking about
selling drugs to little kids and sleeping around
with different girls and then tell me that I'm going to hell for joining a church![8]

I agree with the logic of this young man. Obviously,
there are fine Christian people who are members
of other faiths. I *know* this to be true because one of
my best friends through high school was a rock-solid
Presbyterian who kept the same standards that his LDS
friends did. So let's just assume that this story is an ex-
treme example, and a misunderstanding of what their
own minister said.

It doesn't make sense to me that just because someone belonged to one denomination, they could do or
say whatever they wanted, while others in a different
church who maintained a higher standard would be
bound for hell. That doesn't sound like a God of justice and mercy. What *does* make sense to me is that the
Savior loves people in all religions and honors them
when they follow the light they have received, which

is clearly what He asked them to do. He said, "Come, follow me" (Luke 18:22). He asked, "Why call ye me, Lord, Lord, and do not the things which I say?" (Luke 6:46). He also said, "If ye love me, keep my commandments" (John 14:15). Jesus connected faith to faithfulness. That's logical; it makes sense. And the logic of our doctrine feeds my testimony.

When It Doesn't Make Sense

What do we do when something doesn't fit? Is the whole gospel false because one thing doesn't seem to make sense? Would you throw out all of the wonderful feelings, experiences, and evidences because something you heard doesn't add up? My friend Mark Ellison explained:

> When I was a kid, our family assembled one of those multi-million piece jigsaw puzzles on the dining room table over a period of several weeks. It was a picture of a harbor, with boats at a dock and several beach houses, and also—isn't this always the case?—about twelve square miles of clear, blue sky. "Real good puzzle," we all said. We started assembling the borders—they're

easy. Next, the pieces with parts of the picture fell into place. But then we were left with several bazillion seemingly identical pieces of blue sky. What do you do in a situation like that? If a piece won't fit anywhere, you throw it in the trash, right? "That piece is a hoax!" you say. "In fact, this whole puzzle is a fraud!" Of course, you don't do that. If a piece won't fit anywhere you try it, you set it aside in the "Doesn't Fit Yet" pile. You come back to it later and try again. Voila! It fits, and you say, "Why didn't I see that before?"[9]

Earlier I mentioned the young woman who said, "I don't have a testimony of everything, but I have a testimony of enough." Yes, there will always be new things to learn, and therefore, new things to gain your own witness of—but don't be discouraged. Even Nephi once said, "I know that [God] loveth his children; nevertheless, *I do not know* the meaning of all things" (1 Nephi 11:17, emphasis added). In a talk that you absolutely must read on this topic, Elder Jeffrey R. Holland reassured:

> Please don't hyperventilate if from time to time issues arise that need to be examined,

understood and resolved. They do and they will. In this Church, what we know will always trump what we do not know. And remember, in this world, everyone is to walk by faith.[10]

I suspect that just about everyone in the Church has a "doesn't fit yet" pile or a "back burner" upon which to place things they don't yet understand. I myself have a list of questions to ask the Lord if and when I get the chance! But beneath it all, I believe. And I believe that the time will come when it will all make perfect sense to me. President Spencer W. Kimball wrote, "If you cannot understand fully today, wait patiently and truth will unfold and light will come."[11]

Question Your Doubts

I received an email from a young woman who said in a panic, "I'm starting to question my faith!" I gave her the basic response, "Go see your bishop." But I added, "In the meantime, perhaps you should start questioning your doubts instead of your faith."

Make sure you can tell the difference between doubts and questions. Sometimes we have both, but beneath it all, there's an assurance that the answer is out there. We just need to find it.

One time after a conference, a young woman gave me a thank-you note. She explained that she had been having some doubts about her testimony, but the more she explained, the more I could "read between the lines" that she wasn't so much doubting the Church as she was doubting herself. She had made some mistakes, and the thought of confronting and facing her past was so painful that it was easier to conclude, "Well, maybe the Church isn't true anyway."

Yes, facing our mistakes is difficult, but I believe she wasn't seeing the Church for what it is. The gospel is not just a list of do's and don'ts, or a set of standards and rules to live by. It's not a club for people without problems. The gospel of Jesus Christ is where we go *with* all our mistakes and problems to be forgiven! That is the good news. Jesus Christ came to save sinners, and all of us need Him. One of my favorite "sermons in a sentence" is only five words long. Read it slowly: "I, the Lord, forgive sins" (D&C 61:2). The gospel is not about guilt, it's about hope! If you've ever felt like this young woman, please don't let doubts about your ability to live the gospel get in the way of your quest for a testimony.

Divine Gospel with Human Leaders

Some critics of the Church try to create doubt by discrediting the Church's leaders. If you look for faults in Church leaders, past and present, local and general, you'll find them. If you look for problems in the way things have happened in your branch, ward, or stake, you'll find them, too. Congratulations, you have discovered what we already know: none of us are perfect. I appreciate the experience of Brother Robert L. Millet:

> Many years ago I attended a symposium where a number of presentations on the restored gospel were made, some of which were fairly critical of our faith and way of life. One man, a convert to the Church, spent the first two-thirds of his talk quipping about all of the silly, nonsensical, embarrassing, and even bizarre things that had happened to him since he became a Latterday Saint. The crowd roared. The laughter over the Church and its programs was cruel, painful

to hear, but nonstop for almost an hour. Then the speaker became sober and said, in essence, "Now all of this is quite hilarious, isn't it? There are really some dumb things that happen within Mormonism. There are matters for me that just don't add up, unchristian behaviors that really sting, and situations that need repair. I think we all agree on that. But now let me get to the meat of the matter: I have spent many years of my life studying religions, investigating Christian and non-Christian faiths, immersing myself in their literature and participating in their worship. I have seen it all, from top to bottom and from back to front. And guess what—there's nothing out there that will deal with your questions, solve your dilemmas, or satisfy your soul. This [the restored gospel] is all there is. If there is a true church, this is it. And so you and I had better get comfortable with what we have."[12]

Be sure to recognize the difference between the *people* in the Church and the *teachings* of the Church. It would be pretty pointless to build temples all over the world if they were only intended for perfect people, because we're fresh out of those. Not one person could attend the temple!

If you have doubts about people, that's one thing. If you have doubts or questions about the teachings of the Church, that's another—but it's okay. There will always be a tussle between "belief" and "unbelief," and that is a good thing. We become stronger in a tussle. We gain strength by wrestling with things, and our conviction becomes stronger. Paul said, "Prove all things; hold fast that which is good" (1 Thessalonians 5:21). He did not say, "Accept everything without question." No, we don't have to do that. Put the Lord and His gospel to the test—"prove me now herewith" (Malachi 3:10), the Lord said, and the truths and doctrines of the gospel will pass the test of reason and logic and add to your light.

Some questions simply will not be answered in this life. Do you have questions about dinosaurs? I do. Do you have questions about how the earth was made? I do. Do you have questions about the age of the earth? I do. (It reminds me of another riddle—If you make a cake using flour that is one year old, sugar that is two years old, eggs that are one week old, and milk that is one day old, how old is the cake?) I have many, many questions! But some answers will have to wait. The Lord knows the answers, and one day He'll tell us everything, yes, *everything*. The scriptures promise that He will!

> Yea, verily I say unto you, in that day when the Lord shall come, he shall reveal all things— things which have passed, and hidden things which no man knew, things of the earth, by which it was made, and the purpose and the end thereof—things most precious, things that are above, and things that are beneath, things that are in the earth, and upon the earth, and in heaven. (D&C 101:32–34)

I find comfort in knowing many things about the gospel that make sense. They are logical. I also find comfort in knowing that the Lord knows the answers to all my million questions—even to the things that don't make sense right now. I believe He wants to see what we will do when we *don't* know all the answers. Will we let what we don't know paralyze us so that we don't act on what we do know? No. We will do what Nephi did, "And I was led by the Spirit, *not knowing* beforehand . . ." (1 Nephi 4:6; emphasis added). For me, I know what I know, and what I know trumps what I don't know.

More LIGHT on the subject . . .

Elder Jeffrey R. Holland: https://www
.lds.org/general-conference/2013/04
/lord-i-believe?lang=eng

Stephen E. Robinson, *Are Mormons Christians?* (Deseret Book, 1991).

Notes

1. Robert J. Matthews, *Selected Writings of Robert J. Matthews: Gospel Scholars Series* (Deseret Book, 1999), 29.

2. Boyd K. Packer, "The Cloven Tongues of Fire," *Ensign*, May 2000, 8.

3. *Teachings of the Prophet Joseph Smith* (Deseret Book, 1976), 324.

4. Kieth Merrill, in *Why I'm a Mormon*, ed. Joseph A. Cannon (Ensign Peak, 2012), 232.

5. *Teachings of the Prophet Joseph Smith*, 275.

6. *LDS Church News*, July 4, 1998.

7. "Come Unto Christ," Religion Symposium, Ricks College, January 29, 2000. Available at www2 .byui.edu/presentations/transcripts/religionsymposium/2000_01_29_Bednar.htm

8. Brad Wilcox, *Tips for Tackling Teenage Troubles* (Deseret Book, 1998), 175.

9. Mark Ellison, in *Return with Honor* (Bookcraft, 1995), 92.

10. Jeffrey R. Holland, "Lord, I Believe," *Ensign*, May 2013, 94.

11. Spencer W. Kimball, *President Kimball Speaks Out* (Deseret Book, 1981), 26.

12. Robert L. Millet, *Holding Fast* (Deseret Book, 2008), 134–35.

Let Your Light Shine!

Something wonderful happens when your feelings, your experiences, your evidences, and your logic come together—you glow! When light and truth increase within you, the shine begins to show in your face. This sort of thing happened repeatedly in the scriptures.

For example, when Moses came down from Mount Sinai with the tablets in his hands, "his face shone." In fact, Aaron and the children of Israel "were afraid to come nigh him" because of how he glowed (Exodus 34:29–30). Similarly, when Abinadi testified in King Noah's court, "his face shone with exceeding luster" (Mosiah 13:5), and when missionary brothers Nephi and Lehi were thrown in prison, their faces "did shine exceedingly, even as the faces of angels" (Helaman 5:36).

Watts Up?

Do those "shiny face" stories happen today? Yes, they do, or at least something similar. If you're not sure of the brightness of your own testimony, you may be surprised to know that others see the light in you. They may say, "She glows, she just doesn't know that she glows." A ticket agent at the Dallas/Forth Worth airport commented to a Young Women leader about the group of youth she was sending to Especially for Youth, "I've never seen so many bright eyes." Bright eyes? Hmmm. That's one way to describe it. Here's another—from a sister missionary who served on Temple Square:

> At one point in the tour one of the [Argentine] women looked at me and started gesturing up and down with her hand while saying something [in Spanish] about what I looked like, I guess. I just looked at my companion who had a big smile on her face. Then the woman did the same thing to my companion. Afterwards, my companion filled me in on what the woman

had said. She told us that we looked like we were shining. She wondered what it was about all of us that made us shiny. And she wanted it.[1]

One of my favorite stories in this regard involves Gladys Knight, a Grammy award-winning recording artist who joined the Church. While she was fielding questions during a performance at Disney World, someone noticed—and asked—about her glow:

"I have been a fan of yours for many years. Yet lately you have had a greater light about you. Could you please share with us how this happened?" Now we had a very mixed audience that night—many different ages, races, and religious backgrounds. Attempting to be diplomatic, I answered something like this: "I have learned more about God's standards or commandments that, if obeyed, bring greater peace and happiness. It's not enough to just talk about them, as so many people do. I am now striving more than ever to live them."

Afterward, several other career-oriented questions came up. Then the director said, "We have two roving microphones in the audience.

We'll just take a few more moments for those who would like to ask some more questions."

One of the first people to stand up was a tall, beautiful African-American woman sitting near the front. After receiving a microphone she said, "I am the one who asked about the light you now have. Could you please tell us more specifically how you got that light?"

The question was direct. So I gave a direct answer: "I have become a member of The Church of Jesus Christ of Latter-day Saints." To the surprise of some of my friends watching the show, the audience suddenly burst into applause.[2]

A law professor from Japan visiting the United States spent part of his time at Brigham Young University. Elder Bruce C. Hafen, while serving as an administrator at the university, reported:

After being on the BYU campus several days, mixing in the dorms with students, he said, "You must tell me about these students and their families. This feels like an island of hope in the time of the apocalypse. What is the secret behind all the shining eyes?"[3]

Perhaps someone has seen you in this way. When you have the Spirit with you, when you enjoy its fruits—joy, peace, contentment—it looks like "light" to people who see you. And they want it too! But it's not found in the cosmetics aisle. The plastic surgeon can't give it to you. It's "not available in any stores," as the commercials say. Sister Elaine Dalton taught:

> Deep beauty is the kind of beauty that *shines from the inside out*. It is the kind of beauty that cannot be painted on, surgically created, or purchased. It is the kind of beauty that doesn't wash off. It is *spiritual* attractiveness. Deep beauty springs from virtue. It is the beauty of being chaste and morally clean. It is the kind of beauty that you see in the eyes of virtuous women like your mother and grandmother. It is a beauty that is earned through faith, repentance, and honoring covenants.[4]

President Brigham Young explained it like this: "Those who have got the forgiveness of their sins have countenances that look bright, and they will shine with the intelligence of heaven."[5]

Perhaps you weren't aware of this light within

yourself, but I'll bet your leaders see it. Have they ever welcomed you to church or seminary with, "It's so good to see your bright, smiling faces"? You may encounter the question on your mission, and if anyone ever asks you what that "light" is, you can sing the answer:

> There is sunshine in my soul today,
> More glorious and bright
> Than glows in any earthly sky,
> For Jesus is my light.[6]

Interestingly, the Savior told us that it wasn't enough to bask in our own light. Our dimmer switch isn't intended only for personal use. It's nice to shine, but we've been called to "shine *forth* . . ." (D&C 115:5; emphasis added). Jesus taught:

> Ye are the light of the world. A city that is set on an hill cannot be hid. Neither do men light a candle, and put it under a bushel, but on a candlestick; and it giveth light unto all that are in the house. Let your light so shine before men, that they may see your good works, and glorify your Father which is in heaven. (Matthew 5:14–16)

As I'm sure you know, you don't have to wait until your mission to let your light shine. Wherever you go, you radiate what you are. You cannot hide it, just like you cannot hide a "city on a hill." Whether you open your mouth or not, you are a walking evidence of the truthfulness, the fruits, and the light of the gospel.

What Should I Say if I *Don't* Know That I Know?

As a bishop, I listen more intently to testimonies on fast Sunday than I used to. I want to know if my ward members know, and I'm curious as to *how* they came to know. I am particularly excited when teenagers come up to the stand, and I am just as thrilled when they say "I believe" as I am when they say "I know." Do not ever be embarrassed or ashamed if you feel your level of light is small but growing. There is nothing wrong with saying, "I *hope* the Church is true," or "I *believe* the Church is true," or "I *want* to believe!" Elder Jeffrey R. Holland recalled:

> A 14-year-old boy recently said to me a little hesitantly, "Brother Holland, I can't say yet that I know the Church is true, but I believe it is." I hugged that boy until his eyes bulged out. I told

him with all the fervor of my soul that belief is
a precious word, an even more precious act, and
he need never apologize for "only believing." . . .
I told this boy that belief was always the first step
toward conviction and that the definitive articles of our collective faith forcefully reiterate the
phrase "We believe." And I told him how very
proud I was of him for the honesty of his quest.[7]

I appreciate that Elder Holland praised the boy for
the "honesty of his quest." When I was in Primary, I remember learning the thirteenth article of faith, which
begins, "We believe in being honest . . ." Because of
that article of faith, I felt I couldn't stand up and say I
knew something was true when I really wasn't sure if I
knew. But I believed, and I still believe today.

I repeat what Elder Holland said: "belief is a precious word." King Benjamin must have agreed. He pled
with his people to believe:

Believe in God, believe that he is, and that
he created all things, both in heaven and in
earth; believe that he has all wisdom, and all
power, both in heaven and in earth; believe that

man doth not comprehend all the things which the Lord can comprehend. (Mosiah 4:9)

Some things I believe so strongly that my belief crosses borders with "I'm sure," or "I'm so convinced," into "I know."

Discern between What You Believe and What You Know

Perhaps you're saying at this point, "Okay, Brother Bytheway, I realize now that I've had more witnesses of the Spirit than I thought I had, but I'm still not sure I can say 'I know it's true.'" Fair enough. But I still suggest that you know more than you think you do.

In this book, I've used the metaphor of a dimmer switch or a light for a testimony, since the scriptures often refer to *light* and *knowledge* as synonyms. Alma, however, spoke of planting a seed, and of nourishing it with patience, faith, and diligence until it becomes a tree (see Alma 32). But even Alma couldn't resist bringing the word *light* into the discussion. Watch for the words *enlightened* and *light* as Alma speaks about nurturing the seed:

Ye know that the word hath swelled your souls, and ye also know that it hath sprouted up, that your understanding doth begin to be enlightened, and your mind doth begin to expand. O then, is not this real? I say unto you, Yea, because it is light; and whatsoever is light, is good, because it is discernible, therefore ye must know that it is good. (Alma 32:34–35)

There is a phrase in that verse that I just love—and I think it might help any teenager who wonders if he or she knows the Church is true. Here it is: "Whatsoever is light, is good, because it is *discernible*." I love the word *discernible*. It means "you can tell the difference." A pitch-black room is transformed with the tiniest candle. The difference is discernible. You may not think you know a whole lot about the gospel, but you know some things for sure. You *know* that it is good. Alma said, "If it be a true seed, *or a good seed*" (Alma 32:28; emphasis added). Even if you don't know it is true, you know that it is good. You know that the gospel is good—that it teaches good things, that it produces good people. You know there is goodness there. That is a beginning. And you know more.

You know the feeling in the temple is different from the feeling at the movie theater. It is *discernible*. You know that reading the scriptures feels different from reading just about any other book. It is *discernible*. You know that being in a righteous home feels different from being at a party where bad things are beginning to happen. It is *discernible*. It's a perfect starting point if you need one.

If you're not sure what you know and what you don't know, a wonderful little exercise is to take out a piece of paper and write, "What I Know for Sure" at the top. You might also make a column for "What I Believe" or "What I Hope For." Then just start filling it out. As you list these insights, as you "name them one by one," it just might "surprise you what the Lord has done."[8] Sure, you may not have a testimony of everything, but you will likely discover that you have a testimony of enough—enough to keep going, to keep trying, to keep following Christ to greater light.

Keep the Power Flowing

A testimony is not like riding a bike, where once you've got it figured out, you've always got it figured out. Going back to our metaphor of light, little children see the switch there by the doorway but not the wires concealed by the wall. Those of us who pay the power bill know where the electricity comes from. The light may be generated from heat produced by coal or it may be from a hydroelectric dam or some other source, but the point is, someone is working to send the power. Testimonies require maintenance. Without someone working to ensure a constant flow of power, they may dwindle, becoming dim and weak. President Harold B. Lee taught:

> Testimony isn't something you have today, and you will have always. A testimony is fragile. It is as hard to hold as a moonbeam. It is something you have to recapture every day of your life.[9]

Why did the Lord make it so hard? Why doesn't He just come out and tell the whole world the gospel is true in a dramatic way? Elder Robert L. Simpson suggested that if the Lord were to emblazon the name of the true church in neon letters across the sky, we might pack people in by the thousands, at least for one Sunday. He continued:

There's only one thing wrong with that plan. A week from Saturday night they would be out looking for another miracle to see if they had to go to church again tomorrow. If people come into this church through a miracle, it's a miracle if they stay in the church.[10]

Someone once said, "That which we obtain too easily, we esteem too lightly." A testimony requires work to get and work to keep, which is one reason it is so valuable. The Lord designed it that way, perhaps so that we wouldn't be forced to believe but would choose to believe. If the truths of the gospel were too obvious, it wouldn't require faith to believe in them.

In the meantime, we can believe on the testimony of others as we continue to cultivate our own light. That's what President Boyd K. Packer did when he was young:

> I did not then have a firm testimony that the gospel was true, but I knew that my seminary teachers, Abel S. Rich and John P. Lillywhite, knew it was true. I had heard them testify, and I believed them. I thought to myself, "I will lean

on their testimonies until I gain one of my own."
And so it was.[11]

Heber C. Kimball commented that "The time will
come when no man or woman will be able to endure
on borrowed light."[12] And while it is true that we cannot live on "borrowed light" forever, believing on the
testimony of others is not a cop-out. It is a legitimate
stepping-stone. In fact, the scriptures list it as a spiritual gift! What's more, the scriptures promise eternal
life to those who believe on the testimony of others
and continue faithful. The scriptures teach:

> To some it is given by the Holy Ghost to
> know that Jesus Christ is the Son of God, and
> that he was crucified for the sins of the world. To
> others it is given to believe on their words, that
> they also might have eternal life if they continue
> faithful. (D&C 46:13–14)

Elder Jeffrey R. Holland invited those who are still
searching to "believe on his words," or to lean on his
testimony:

> What was once a tiny seed of belief for me
> has grown into the tree of life, so if your faith is a

little tested in this or any season, I invite you to lean on mine.[13]

Now, what do we do as we move forward? Whether your testimony is a tiny light, or as bright as the sun, you have to keep it going. To fan the flame of your faith, give it your ALL—Ask, Learn, and Live.

Keep Asking. You are reading this book because a teenage boy asked a question in 1820. Never underestimate the power of a teenager's question. The scriptures encourage us to ask and to ask often. For example, "Ask, and ye shall receive" (D&C 4:7), "Whatsoever things ye shall ask the Father in my name shall be given unto you" (3 Nephi 27:28), and "Ye have not, because ye ask not" (James 4:2).

Continue asking. I suggest that *every time* you say a personal prayer, you ask your Father in Heaven to strengthen your testimony, to give you a witness of the Spirit, and to help you recognize those you have already received. That's what I do. And I am going to keep asking that, every day. Joseph Smith once said, "Weary [the Lord] until he blesses you."[14] Wonderful things happen if you keep asking. With few exceptions, every revelation given in the Doctrine and Covenants was given as a result of someone asking the Lord a question through prayer. Elder D. Todd Christofferson pleaded with the youth of the Church to keep asking:

> I promise you, young people, that if you will continue faithful, asking, the Lord is going to give you the same answer, the same testimony, the same confirmation that He gave me, because I know that He loves all of you as much as He does me or President Thomas S. Monson or any one of His children. God's love is for everyone, and it is infinite. He knows how to communicate with each person. He knows where you are and how to reach your heart and spirit through the Holy Spirit. Do not stop praying. Do not stop asking. Do not stop obeying the commandments. The time will come, if it has not already, when you will receive this strong testimony. And it will not be just once. But rather, through the Lord's mercy, it will come time after time after time throughout your life.[15]

Keep Learning. We will never run out of new things to learn. The gospel is so full that we'll never comprehend it all in this life. (But it sure is fun to try!) You can't gain a testimony of a principle you know nothing about. But as you learn new things, the Spirit can confirm to your heart and mind the truth of those new things. Thus, the more you know, the more your testimony can grow, and the brighter it becomes. This is why it is vital to attend seminary, and to go to your weekly Church meetings, and to engage in personal study. Every meeting is another chance to gain new light and knowledge.

And for maximum light, focus your learning on the best things. Jesus taught, "Learn of *me*, and listen to *my* words . . ." (D&C 19:23; emphasis added). Notice, we're supposed to study *His* words. It's always safer to read what Jesus said than to read what others think about what Jesus said. Similarly, it's always safer to read what the Mormons themselves say they believe than to read what our critics say we believe.

I suppose we've all encountered anti-Mormon literature and experienced the dark feelings it brings. (Hmmm, if it makes you feel dark and hollow, what do you think that means?) When I was growing up, there was a song called "Looking for Love in All the Wrong Places." We make a similar mistake if we look for *light* in the *dark*. If you have questions, that's good. We all do. Just be sure to ask someone you trust, starting with the Lord Himself. Oddly enough, some people, when they begin to doubt, move away from prayer and scripture study instead of moving toward God with their questions. Strangely, they are looking for light in the dark. When I was young, and I felt my faith being shaken, I discovered that if I would just spend a few minutes reading the Book of Mormon, I felt its power, the lights came back on, and I could sense that I had returned to solid ground.

Keep Living the Gospel. Asking is good, but asking and doing is better. It won't hurt to repeat again what Jesus said, "If any man will do his [the Father's] will, he shall know of the doctrine, whether it be of God, or whether I speak of myself" (John 7:17). When you are living the gospel, the fruits of the gospel can and will grow in your life, providing experiences and evidences of the truth.

When I was in the Missionary Training Center, I spent many hours in the custodial closets at night praying for a stronger testimony. It never came in the MTC. But it did come. I felt stronger witnesses while teaching

the gospel as a missionary than I did in the broom closets. Based on that experience, I believe that more testimonies come to people while they are sharing what
they know than while they are sitting and waiting for
a witness to come in some other way. Brigham Young
put it this way: "More people have received testimonies on their feet than down on their knees praying for
them."[16] In other words, they are out doing the work
instead of merely praying about the work. Don't misunderstand, the praying is important—but prayer plus
action is more likely to result in testimony.

President Boyd K. Packer taught we must go to the
edge of our light to find more light:

> A testimony is to be *found* in the *bearing* of it.
> Somewhere in your quest for spiritual knowledge,
> there is that "leap of faith," as the philosophers
> call it. It is the moment when you have gone to
> the edge of the light and step into the darkness
> to discover that the way is lighted ahead for just
> a footstep or two. . . . It is one thing to receive
> a witness from what you have read or what an-
> other has said; and that is a necessary beginning.
> It is quite another to have the Spirit confirm to

you in your bosom that what *you* have testified is true. Can you not see that it will be supplied as you share it? As you give that which you have, there is a replacement, with increase![17]

As you prepare for your mission, be where you are supposed to be, and be doing what you are supposed to be doing. You will discover that the simple standards outlined in *For the Strength of Youth* will help you find the maximum possible joy and happiness. You will enjoy the fruits of the gospel as you live the standards, and if you keep your eyes open, you will also witness in the lives of others what happens when they don't. They will also reap what they sow. Over time, you will go from knowing the standards are "good" and "wise" to knowing they are true, because of their fruits.

What I Know for Sure

In closing, let me tell you what I know. I know by the *feelings* I have felt that there is a God. When I pray, when I read about Him, when I ask Him for help, I feel it. I really believe someone is there. It is discernible.

I know that the Book of Mormon is true. When I read it and study it I know, by the feelings I have felt, that it is true and reliable. I've also learned that it is as deep as it is wide. It is solid and profound and powerful and it points me to Jesus Christ, who is my Savior. The Doctrine and Covenants blows me away. To hear the voice of the Lord in modern times is amazing. To have the Lord add to our knowledge and give us more light beyond what we have in ancient scripture is so exciting. One of the first times I felt the Spirit and *knew* that I did was while reading D&C 19:38–41. It was discernible. The Pearl of Great Price carries and conveys the same reverent spirit. It is indeed a treasure. What it reveals about Abraham and Moses, and what they knew, inspires me and makes perfect sense to me too.

I feel the same feelings when I read the Bible. When I read the stories of Jesus, I marvel at the things He said, which often left people amazed and astonished. His teachings were (and are) so simple yet so powerful. His compassion for sinners and for the poor and downtrodden is humbling and motivating at the same time. He really loved people, and He proved it by healing them and weeping with them. I am inspired by His courage to continue His mission, to perform the

Atonement knowing that He would die in a horrible way. His constant focus on doing the Father's will is powerful to me. He is the Son of God. The feelings I feel when I read the Bible testify of its truth. It is discernible.

I know by *experience* that living the gospel brings the sweetest fruit. My greatest joys and my greatest successes in life are a direct result of applying the teachings of the gospel. I know by experience that I am happiest when I try to live close to the Spirit. I also know by experience that I feel miserable when I stray. I know it. It is discernible. I've experienced it over and over and over. How can I deny it?

I am strengthened by the *evidences* that I see all around me. I see the fruits of the gospel almost every day as a teacher. I am strengthened as I meet with teenagers and young adults who stand tall and true, who are happy and bright, and who know who they are and what they want to become. They are so incredibly unusual in this world, and they don't even realize it. I see what the gospel does for people who live it. I see what they become, and it is evidence of the gospel's goodness and truthfulness.

I believe the gospel because of its *logic* and reason. It makes sense to me. It clicks. As I read and study, I encounter new doctrines and principles that I've never heard before. Gospel study is sprinkled with wonderful "aha moments," and each time I study, another piece of the puzzle falls into place. Everything I learn about the plan of salvation points to a loving God who is both just and merciful and who remembers all His children throughout the world in every condition and circumstance. Those who die without hearing the gospel, who never knew anything about Jesus, have the same opportunities that we do because of the restoration of temples and temple work. I see evidence of God's perfect justice and mercy in the plan of salvation that I don't see in any other religion or philosophy I've studied.

Leave the Light On

I know—and most importantly, you can know too. I don't have to say, nor would I ever say, "Just take my word for it." Study it for yourself. Put it into practice, and do His will.

This is the end of the book, but hopefully not

the end of your quest. Is your testimony a little stronger now that you've read this book than it was when you began? I hope so. I wish there were an exact formula for gaining a testimony, complete with a timeline. I wish we could say, "If you do this and this and this, you will know on this date." Too bad there isn't a testimony app! But it doesn't work that way. Elder M. Russell Ballard expressed it like this:

> And how do you get such a testimony? Well, there's no new technology for that, nor will there ever be. You cannot do a Google search to gain a testimony. You can't text message faith. You gain a vibrant, life-changing testimony today the same way it has always been done. The process hasn't been changed. It comes through desire, study, prayer, obedience, and service. That is why the teachings of prophets and apostles, past and present, are as relevant to your life today as they ever have been.[18]

If you are really serious about gaining a stronger testimony, go back and watch and listen to the talks linked to the QR codes at the end of each chapter. I didn't choose them because I liked the look of techie endnotes. I really believe they will help you.

There will be more books to read, more talks to listen to, and more articles to read, all of which will help you come to know the truth. A testimony, like a light, needs a constant flow of power. Pray every day for the feelings, experiences, evidences, and logic that will feed your soul, and the sunshine in your heart will begin to show in your life. "Doubt not, but be believing" (Mormon 9:27), with the assurance that one day you will know, and you will know that you know.

More LIGHT on the subject . . .

 President James E. Faust: https://www
.lds.org/general-conference/2005/10
/the-light-in-their-eyes?lang=eng
&media=video#watch=video

John Bytheway, *Weed Your Brain, Grow Your Testimony*, talk on CD
(Deseret Book, 2008).
Why I Believe (Bookcraft, 2002).
Why I'm a Mormon, ed. Joseph A. Cannon (Ensign Peak, 2012).
www.mormonscholarstestify.org

Notes

1. Personal email from Sister Christensen.

2. Gladys Knight, in *Why I Believe* (Bookcraft, 2002), 187.

3. Bruce C. Hafen, in *Why I Believe*, 159.

4. Elaine S. Dalton, "Remember Who You Are," *Ensign*, May 2010, 122; emphasis added.

5. Brigham Young, in *Times and Seasons*, July 1, 1845, 956.

6. "There Is Sunshine in My Soul Today," *Hymns* (The Church of Jesus Christ of Latter-day Saints, 1985), 227.

7. Jeffrey R. Holland, "Lord, I Believe," *Ensign*, May 2013, 94–95.

8. "Count Your Blessings," *Hymns*, no. 241.

9. *LDS Church News*, April 6, 1975, 11.

10. Robert L. Simpson, in *Testimony*, comp. H. Stephen Stoker and Joseph C. Muren (Bookcraft, 1980), 155.

11. Boyd K. Packer, "Counsel to Youth," *Ensign*, November 2011, 17.

12. Heber C. Kimball, in Orson F. Whitney, *Life of Heber C. Kimball* (Bookcraft, 1945), 449–50.

13. Jeffrey R. Holland, "Lord, I Believe," 95.

14. *The Words of Joseph Smith: The Contemporary Accounts of the Nauvoo Discourses of the Prophet Joseph*, comp. Andrew F. Ehat and Lyndon W. Cook (Bookcraft, 1980), 15.

15. D. Todd Christofferson, "Strong Impressions of the Spirit," *New Era*, June 2013, 4.

16. Brigham Young, as quoted in Leah D. Widtsoe, "'Brigham Young and the Youth Movement,'" *Improvement Era*, June 1935, 384.

17. Boyd K. Packer, *That All May Be Edified* (Bookcraft, 1982), 340; emphasis in original.

18. M. Russell Ballard, "Learning the Lessons of the Past," *Ensign*, May 2009, 34.

Acknowledgments

I am indebted to the entire Deseret Book team for their support and encouragement, especially Lisa Roper, Laurel Day, and Chris Schoebinger. I am also grateful to Brad Wilcox and Lexi Silva for reading the initial manuscript and sharing their ideas. Special thanks to Emily Watts for her editorial skill, suggestions, and friendship.